Marion Campbell.

SPA DINING

Spa DINING

Health Travel International

ST. MARTIN'S PRESS · NEW YORK

Copy Editor: Marjorie Tippie

Design by Mina Greenstein

Library of Congress Cataloging in Publication Data
Main entry under title:
Spa dining.
    Includes index.
    1. Low-carbohydrate diet—Recipes. 2. Salt-free
diet—Recipes. I. Health Travel International.
RM237.73.S68   1985   641.5'635   85-12507
ISBN 0-312-74927-9

First Edition
10 9 8 7 6 5 4 3 2 1

DEDICATION

This book is dedicated to the health spa industry and people everywhere who fight the never-ending diet and fitness battle.

ACKNOWLEDGMENTS

Pam Hoenig's hard work and superior editorial skills were essential ingredients to the completion of this book.

We would like to express our gratitude to the many spas who were kind enough to reveal their "family secrets."

Finally, our special thanks go to Ken Dachman, whose guidance and expertise made this book possible.

CONTENTS

INTRODUCTION

This is an age of fitness enlightenment.

Never before have so many paid so much attention to the health of their bodies. It's not a transient craze, and it's not evidence of runaway self-indulgence. Sensible eating and exercise habits are really preventive medicine—an effective defense against depression, stress, heart attacks, ulcers, and high blood pressure.

Unfortunately, the sincere desire to establish an effective long-term self-health program is too often foiled by the relentless pressures and smothering inertia of our everyday lives. We could use a fresh start, a new look at ourselves, a dramatic push in the right direction, some way to break free of the negative patterns we've been caught up in for far too long.

Health spas offer exactly this kind of life-changing revitalization. Spas take a holistic approach to health; they exist to reshape the body and the mind. Each, you'll find, is unique in its ambience and methods.

Spas have a long and honorable history, dating back to the fifth century B.C. in ancient Greece. Originally, spas were recuperative retreats, usually located near healing mineral springs, and patients went there to seek relief from physical ailments. But the nature of the spa has changed over the centuries. The town of Spa, in Belgium, has been famous for its soothing waters for over four hundred years, and today lends its name to thousands of full-service health resorts throughout the world.

Some spas pamper their guests; others require self-sacrifice. Some spas are plush and expensive; others are comfortably informal and moderately priced. Spas can be found in a myriad of locations: in a Victorian mansion or a metropolitan hotel, in an English castle or a sleepy glen in the foothills of the Adirondacks. Fitness buffs can choose a desert retreat or a North Woods hideaway; take in the sea air at an oceanside spa or work out overlooking an ice-blue midwestern lake.

This book will guide you through a delightful cross-section of popular spas, where you'll be exposed to a kaleidoscopic array of dietary and fitness philosophies. You'll get a good feeling for each spa's atmosphere and attitude, pick up useful exercise tips, and learn intriguing techniques for meal presentation.

Best of all, the spas' highly regarded chefs and dieticians will share some of their tastiest secrets with you—in over three hundred recipes you can use to prepare spa meals in your own kitchen.

For several years now, a trend toward lighter, smarter eating has been gaining strength in this country. Americans have discovered that food need not be smothered in thick, rich sauces to taste terrific. Nutrition, according to one supermarket executive, "has become a genuine media event, a national preoccupation." A report compiled by the National Restaurant Association agreed. "Light nutritious meals have become good business," the report concluded. John Harris, a cookbook publisher, summarized the current state of popular techniques in meal preparation in this perceptive comment: "We've come a long way from steak and potatoes," Harris said. "We've also come a long way from alfalfa sprouts, honey, and granola. The haute cuisine and health food forces have gotten together."

As the recipes collected in this book indicate, spa chefs have anticipated this trend (by a couple of decades in some cases).

In a general sense, you'll find a degree of similarity in many of the spa menus. Fresh fruits and vegetables are plentiful; fat, salt, sugar, and red meat are scarce. Examine the individual recipes, however, and you'll be amazed at the diversity of ingredients and suggestions for preparation. You'll find old favorites done up in fresher, healthier styles and exotic dishes you've probably never considered using in a diet plan.

A convenient meal index concludes the book; use it to design your own "home spa" menus. You'll find breakfasts, soups, salads, entrées, and desserts that you can combine to meet your individual health goals and culinary preferences. Basics such as sauces, soup stocks, and salad dressings are also included. Vegetable dishes abound, and can be used as entrées or side dishes.

Many of the recipes are extremely low in calories; others are a shade less restrictive. All result in satisfying, nutritious meals. Some of the ingredients may not be immediately familiar to you, but all can be found in most large supermarkets, gourmet shops, or health food stores.

To structure a personal spa eating plan, determine the weight you'd like to reach, or maintain. Then use the following formula to calculate the daily caloric limit that will result in that goal weight:

1. Multiply your desired weight by 16 (if you are a woman) or 18 (if you are a man).
2. Subtract 10 calories for each year of age over 22.

It's important to note that this formula assumes a relatively low level of physical activity. By exercising daily, you can, of course, increase your allowable caloric intake. (Walking for thirty minutes daily, for instance, adds about 300 calories to your daily limit.)

Complement your spa diet program by following these general "eating strategies," gleaned from the advice of the experts who operate the world's most successful health resorts:

1. Drink water throughout the day, beginning as soon as you get up. Try to drink 8 glasses daily.
2. Never skip breakfast.
3. Cut down on the use of white sugar, which is high in calories but has no nutritional value.
4. Salt should be used sparingly, if at all. Substitute a vegetable-based seasoning.
5. Use skim milk instead of whole, whipped margarine instead of solid.
6. Cut down on fats. Reduce consumption of meat to 5 to 6 ounces of lean meat daily. Use unsaturated oils and margarine.
7. Cook by steaming, grilling, broiling, roasting, or boiling. Frying, especially deep frying, should be avoided.
8. Use fresh fruits and vegetables to the greatest extent possible. If canned fruit must be used, choose the varieties packed in water or their own juices.
9. Seafood and poultry are much better for you than red meat.
10. Don't overcook your food. Overcooking robs food of valuable nutrients. Be particularly careful with vegetables. Cook until crisp, not soggy.
11. Include some fiber in your daily diet—a salad, a baked potato, whole-grain bread or cereal.
12. Thicken sauces with arrowroot or a purée of vegetables rather than with butter or meat drippings.

13. Eat slowly. Relax. Enjoy.
14. Present meals attractively. Good china, a pleasing combination of colors, and imaginative garnishes make food much more appetizing.

Now read on.

You'll find hundreds of delicious recipes to assist you in staying within your daily caloric limit. And you won't feel deprived.

You will also visit some fascinating resorts and meet some dedicated people whose primary concern is your good health and happiness.

The Golden Door

Long before most Americans discovered "nouvelle cuisine," the contemporary school of low-calorie, low-sodium, low-fat French cooking, Deborah Szekely and her Belgian chef Michel Stroot were serving this style of food to guests at the Golden Door, an exclusive and expensive health spa in Escondido, California, thirty miles from San Diego. Included in the Golden Door's approximately $2,500 weekly charge are all meals, a range of activities to tone both mind and body, and everything necessary for a week's stay except running shoes, bathing suits, and personal items. For guests who elect to wear their own clothes rather than the supply of "spa issue" exercise clothes, ponchos, robes or kimonos, there is a daily laundry service. At the end of the week, each guest receives a cassette tape of exercises tailored to the individual's needs.

As guests cross the wooden footbridge over Deer Springs stream and pass through the solid bronze portals of "the Door," the effect is that of crossing over into a world of tranquility. The original Golden Door, which opened in 1958 and was for women only, closed in 1969 to make room for a freeway. Szekely, the Door's owner, purchased a nearby 157-acre citrus grove and created the present resort, modeled after the traditional Japanese Honjin-style inn, or *ryokan*. Guests stay in three guest houses tastefully decorated with the understated elegance of Oriental art and furnishings, and guests' names are spelled out in gold letters above their rooms.

After check-in and a preliminary interview to determine each individual's needs and goals, the Door's guests assemble for Sunday night dinner, preceded by a get-acquainted cocktail party (nonalcoholic, of course) featuring an assortment of fruit and vegetable drinks and, for munching, crudités and dip.

CRUDITÉS FOR HORS D'OEUVRES

Carrot sticks	Snow peas
Cherry tomatoes	Jícama slices
Turnip slices	Zucchini sticks
Celery sticks	Bell pepper rings
Radish rosettes	Cucumber slices

Lettuce for serving tray

The above will make a tantalizing tray of crudités—a French term meaning "raw." The vegetables should be presented attractively on a bed of lettuce, arranged around a bowl of dip, such as the following.

SAUCE RAIFORT

1/2 cup plain low-fat yogurt
2 tablespoons creamed horseradish
1 tablespoon Dijon mustard
Ground red (cayenne) pepper to taste
Garnish: Thinly sliced radishes or chopped scallions

With a wire whisk, mix all ingredients except radishes or scallions till smooth. Top with radishes or scallions. Use as a dip. Also excellent with baked or broiled fish.

MAKES ABOUT 3/4 CUP. CALORIES PER TABLESPOON: 10

The closeness and camaraderie that are important parts of a stay here begin at the cocktail party and continue to grow during the week, so that many of the guests make plans to meet again—on the outside or back at the Golden Door. Most guests are repeaters, and the Door is a favorite haunt of the wealthy and/or famous. The spa has been visited by such celebrities as Barbra Streisand, Robert Wagner, Kim Novak, Bill Blass, and Craig Claiborne.

Increasingly, in recent years, the Door has hosted seminars for fitness-conscious executives, and several weeks each year are set aside for couples or for men only.

The workout begins early Monday morning with warm-up stretches and a walk before breakfast. For those guests who have chosen to "cleanse" their bodies, Monday is "virtue-making" day, with a 500-calorie, mostly liquid diet.

Individual daily schedules are printed on Japanese fans that guests pin to their clothing, freeing them from the burden of serenity-disturbing decision making. This serenity is achieved by the charming surroundings, the healthful diet, and by balancing strenuous exercise with herbal wraps and massages, and quiet meditations with classes in cooking, nutrition, flower arranging, or stress management. If requested, a newspaper is delivered daily to the guest's room, but this type of reading is discouraged. It's not in keeping with the Golden Door's philosophy of mental and physical purification through a healthful diet and a disciplined regimen.

Szekely encourages guests to set their own pace, especially during difficult workouts like the "Da Vinci" aerobics class (based on the artist's theory of health through tracing circles, points and lines with body movements). She continually looks for ways to improve the Golden Door, and takes an active part in its activities, giving a weekly talk and joining her guests for meals. A midweek favorite is her special brunch.

Brunch with Deborah:

HUEVOS RANCHEROS

2 tablespoons sesame-seed or safflower oil
3 medium-size onions, sliced
1 green bell pepper, seeded and chopped (optional)
1 tablespoon dried oregano
1 tablespoon dried basil
1 teaspoon vegetable salt
1 can (28 ounces) whole tomatoes, chopped, or 4 large
    fresh, ripe tomatoes, peeled and coarsely chopped
1/2 teaspoon freshly ground black pepper
4 eggs, in shell
1/2 cup freshly shredded Monterey Jack cheese or 4 thin
    slices mozzarella cheese

Heat oil in heavy pan. Gently sauté onions over low heat till light golden brown, stirring occasionally with wooden spatula. Add green pepper and season with oregano, basil, and vegetable salt. Sauté another 2 to 3 minutes. Add tomatoes and black pepper. Simmer, uncovered, 10 to 15 minutes, till sauce is somewhat thick.

With spoon, make 4 pockets in mixture; carefully break an egg into each pocket. Cover eggs with cheese. Cook, covered, 10 minutes for soft eggs, 15 minutes for eggs more well done.

Serve immediately.

SERVINGS: 4. CALORIES PER SERVING: 244

Basic to Chef Michel Stroot's recipes is the use of lemon and grapefruit juice, touches of nutmeg, garlic, and quite a lot of cayenne pepper and horseradish to bring out the flavor of foods without using salt. All the fresh herbs, fruits, and vegetables, and even the chickens, Chef Stroot uses are raised on Golden Door grounds. For cooks without access to farming facilities, Chef Stroot suggests growing potted chives and herbs in a windowsill or kitchen garden. He adds small amounts of low-sodium cheeses to salads and stocks to enhance flavors and uses Neufchâtel cheese to "whiten" sauces. The effort involved in preparing these basic sauces, dressings, and stocks is slight; the gastronomical rewards are great.

LEMON DRESSING

1/4 cup sesame-seed or safflower oil
3 tablespoons lemon juice
2 tablespoons chopped fresh parsley
1/2 teaspoon vegetable salt
1/4 teaspoon freshly ground black pepper
2 to 3 tablespoons freshly grated Parmesan or Romano
    cheese

Place all ingredients except cheese in blender. Blend till parsley is finely chopped. Add cheese when tossing salad.

MAKES ABOUT 3/4 CUP. CALORIES PER TABLESPOON: 96

Note: To preserve fresh lemon flavor, prepare this dressing just before serving.

MAYONNAISE

2 teaspoons Dijon mustard
1 egg yolk
2 shallots, chunked (about 4 teaspoons)
1 teaspoon freshly ground black pepper
2 tablespoons cider vinegar or lemon juice
1/2 cup sesame-seed or safflower oil

Put all ingredients except oil in blender. Blend until smooth, then, with motor running slowly, add oil to thicken.
    MAKES ABOUT 1 CUP. CALORIES PER TABLESPOON: 67

MAYONETTE SAUCE

1 cup Mayonnaise (see preceding recipe)
1/2 cup plain low-fat yogurt

Combine in blender until smooth.
    MAKES 1 1/2 CUPS. CALORIES PER TABLESPOON: 58

SAUCE MADRAS (CURRY)

1 teaspoon safflower oil
1 tablespoon finely chopped shallots
1 to 2 teaspoons curry powder
1 cup Mayonette Sauce (see preceding recipe)
1/2 ripe banana
Ground red (cayenne) pepper to taste

Heat oil in small skillet. Add shallots and sauté lightly over low heat till they are glazed. Add curry powder. Mix with wooden spatula to make a paste, taking care not to burn the curry powder. Combine curry mixture, banana, and mayonette in blender; blend until smooth. Add dash of cayenne. Use this sauce to coat broccoli, cauliflower, or cabbage. Also nice with seafood.

MAKES ABOUT 2 CUPS. CALORIES PER TABLESPOON: 62

VEGETABLE STOCK

1 whole celery stalk or 1 small celery root, trimmed
1 onion, peeled, studded with 4 cloves
2 leeks (white part only), thoroughly cleaned
1 carrot, trimmed
4 fresh, ripe tomatoes, quartered
1 small turnip, trimmed
1 teaspoon dried thyme
2 bay leaves
10 peppercorns, crushed
12 cups water
2 tablespoons low sodium soy sauce
1 tablespoon sea salt

Combine all ingredients in large stockpot. Slowly bring to boil. Simmer, uncovered, about 2 hours, reducing liquid to about 10 cups. Strain through cheesecloth before using.

MAKES ABOUT 10 CUPS. CALORIES PER CUP: 11

VICHYSOISSE

2 teaspoons safflower oil
3 leeks (white part only), thoroughly cleaned and coarsely
    chopped (about 1 1/4 cups)
1 large onion, finely chopped
2 potatoes, peeled, diced, and rinsed
1 fresh thyme sprig (or 1/4 teaspoon dried thyme)
1 bay leaf
3 1/2 cups Vegetable Stock (see preceding recipe)
3 ounces Neufchâtel cheese
Vegetable salt to taste
Freshly grated nutmeg to taste
Garnish: 1/4 cup finely chopped chives or scallions

Heat oil in heavy saucepan and gently sauté leeks and onion
till slightly glazed. Add potatoes, thyme, and bay leaf. Steam,
covered, over low heat 8 to 10 minutes. Add vegetable stock.
Simmer, covered, 40 minutes, or till vegetables are tender.
    Cool. Discard thyme (if fresh sprig was used) and bay
leaf. Combine mixture with cheese in blender; blend till
smooth and creamy. Season with vegetable salt, then chill.
Sprinkle with nutmeg and garnish with chives to serve.
    SERVINGS: 4 TO 8. CALORIES PER SERVING: 73 TO 146

FISH BOUILLON

2 pounds fish heads, bones, and trimmings
3 quarts water
Bouquet garni, consisting of following ingredients bound
    in cheesecloth:
3 whole celery stalks, trimmed
1 bay leaf
1 teaspoon dried thyme

2 or 3 fresh parsley sprigs
10 peppercorns, crushed
2 teaspoons sea salt
1 whole carrot, trimmed

Combine all ingredients in stockpot. Simmer gently, uncovered, 2 to 3 hours, until liquid is reduced to 6 to 8 cups. Be sure to skim foam. Strain through cheesecloth before using.

MAKES 6 TO 8 CUPS. CALORIES PER CUP: 25 TO 30

Almost as important to the Golden Door plan as the food itself are the rituals surrounding its consumption. A vase of fresh flowers adorns each breakfast tray. Several courses of small portions are served on attractive plates. Szekely suggests eating lunch in two shifts—taking a ten-minute conversation break in midmeal to allow the blood sugar level to rise, thus helping to control the appetite. The cocktail hour before dinner serves the same purpose. Exercising before meals will raise the metabolism rate, burning more calories. And always, always, she admonishes, eat slowly, chewing each bite forty times, savoring the taste, and enjoying a relaxed atmosphere created just for mealtime pleasure.

A week at the Golden Door is a week of pampering. There are more than three staff members for each guest, providing services from running errands to town to "movement assessment" by a qualified physical therapist. And, of course, there is the food—prepared with excellence and served with grace—whether it be breakfast, lunch, or dinner, main course or dessert.

BROILED GRAPEFRUIT

1 grapefruit, pink or white
2 teaspoons brown sugar, firmly packed
Pinch ground ginger
Garnish: 2 fresh strawberries, halved

Preheat oven to 375 degrees.
    Halve grapefruit. Use knife to cut out center membrane and loosen grapefruit segments. Sprinkle with sugar and ginger. Place in a baking pan and bake 15 minutes or till bubbly and very hot. Place berries in center and serve immediately.
    SERVINGS: 2. CALORIES PER SERVING: 65

PAPAYA AND COTTAGE CHEESE

2 ripe papayas
1 cup low-fat cottage cheese
1 cup unprocessed bran
4 teaspoons raw sunflower seeds
Garnish: Strawberries and fresh mint sprigs

Halve papayas; scrape out and discard seeds. Fill each papaya half with 1/4 cup low-fat cottage cheese. Sprinkle top with bran and sunflower seeds. Garnish with strawberries and mint and serve.
    SERVINGS: 4. CALORIES PER SERVING: 103

BRAN BREAKFAST

1/2 cup unprocessed bran
1/4 cup raw wheat germ

1/4 cup raw sunflower seeds
4 teaspoons sun-dried raisins
Ground cinnamon to taste

Combine all ingredients and mix well.
SERVINGS: 4. CALORIES PER SERVING: 103
Note: Top with 1/2 cup unfiltered apple juice or other
juice of your choice—i.e., apricot, pear, grapefruit—or 1/4
cup low-fat milk or plain low-fat yogurt.

EVERYWOMAN'S DIET PLATE

2 hard-cooked eggs
1 teaspoon Dijon mustard
Pinch vegetable salt
1 teaspoon Neufchâtel cheese
1/2 teaspoon dried oregano
1 cup low-fat cottage cheese
2 fresh, ripe tomatoes, sliced
1 head Bibb lettuce
Garnish: 1 tablespoon raw sunflower seeds

Slice eggs in half. Remove yolks and put into small bowl
along with mustard, vegetable salt, and Neufchâtel cheese;
mash together with a fork till smooth. Fill egg cavities with
yolk filling. Mix oregano into cottage cheese. Arrange eggs,
cheese mixture, and sliced tomatoes over lettuce on 2 plates.
Garnish with sunflower seeds and serve.
SERVINGS: 2. CALORIES PER SERVING: 90

CRAB-STUFFED PAPAYA

2 large ripe papayas (about 1 pound each), halved length-
    wise and seeded
3/4 pound king crabmeat, cooked and shredded
1 1/2 teaspoons curry powder
3 tablespoons finely chopped fresh chives
2 tablespoons raw sunflower seeds
2 teaspoons lemon juice
Lettuce leaves to line 4 plates
Garnish: Lemon wedges and fresh vegetables, such as
    julienned green beans, snow peas (blanched), red
    bell pepper rings, cherry tomatoes, or shredded
    carrots

With small melon-ball scoop, remove most of papaya from
shells, leaving only enough to give shells stability. Place
papaya balls in bowl. Add crab, curry powder, chives, sunflower seeds, and lemon juice and mix thoroughly. Spoon
filling into papaya shells.
    Place papaya shells on 4 beds of lettuce. Garnish with
lemon wedges and whatever fresh vegetables with compati-
ble flavor and color you have on hand, and serve.
    SERVINGS: 4. CALORIES PER SERVING: 167

TUNA SALAD

1 can (13 ounces) solid white tuna in water, drained
1/2 cup low-fat cottage cheese
2 tablespoons minced shallots or white part of scallions
2 tablespoons Mustard Vinaigrette Dressing (recipe
    follows)
2 tablespoons chopped celery
2 tablespoons chopped fresh parsley
1 tablespoon lemon juice

Salad greens to line 4 plates
Garnish: Tomato wedges, lemon wedges, parsley sprigs,
      radish roses

Crumble tuna and mix with cottage cheese. Combine shallots
and dressing; add to tuna. Add celery, parsley, and lemon
juice; mix well. Spoon onto 4 beds of greens. Garnish and
serve.

SERVINGS: 4. CALORIES PER SERVING: 144

MUSTARD VINAIGRETTE DRESSING

1 tablespoon Dijon mustard
1 teaspoon freshly ground black pepper
5 1/2 tablespoons cider vinegar
6 1/2 tablespoons safflower oil
1 tablespoon water

Mix together all ingredients in an 8-ounce jar. Before using,
close lid tightly and shake vigorously.

MAKES ABOUT 1 CUP. CALORIES PER TABLESPOON: 59

Note: A strong dressing, this should be used sparingly. It
keeps well under refrigeration.

TROPICAL TURKEY SALAD

4 small heads Bibb lettuce
1 small apple with skin, thinly sliced
8 cooked turkey slices (about 1 1/2 to 1 3/4 each)
Garnish: 8 thinly sliced radishes, 4 pitted and sliced black
      olives, 1 bunch watercress, 4 lemon wedges
1/2 cup Mustard Vinaigrette Dressing (see preceding
      recipe)
1/2 cup chopped ripe mango (or pineapple or pear)
2 teaspoons lemon juice

Place leaves from 1 head of lettuce in center of each of 4 chilled salad plates. Arrange 4 apple slices and 2 turkey slices around lettuce. Garnish.

Mix dressing, mango, and lemon juice in blender. Serve this dressing on side; pour up to 1 tablespoon over each serving of turkey and apples.

SERVINGS: 4. CALORIES PER SERVING: 214

CHICKEN SALAD USU ZUKURI

1 teaspoon safflower oil
1 large clove garlic, minced
2 whole chicken breasts, split (about 3 1/2 ounces per
    serving)
2 tablespoons minced shallots
2 teaspoons low-sodium soy sauce
2 tablespoons lemon juice
3 teaspoons minced lemon zest
2 tablespoons minced fresh ginger
5 ounces tofu
Lettuce leaves to line 4 plates
Garnish: Radish slices, mung beans, cucumber slices
    (peeled), julienned carrots, chopped fresh tomatoes

Preheat oven to 350 degrees.

Heat oil in 6-inch skillet. Gently sauté garlic 1 to 2 minutes; stir frequently. Add chicken breasts, skin side down. Sprinkle shallots around them. Cook breasts 2 to 3 minutes on each side, till golden brown; shake pan if necessary to prevent chicken from sticking. Pour soy sauce and lemon juice over chicken. Add ginger and 2 teaspoons of the lemon zest. Turn breasts till completely coated with sauce. Bake, covered, 25 to 30 minutes.

Remove pan from oven. Remove chicken breasts to plate to cool; reserve 2 tablespoons of the pan juices.

While breasts are cooling, prepare tofu sauce. Place tofu,

remaining 1 teaspoon lemon zest, and reserved pan juices in blender. Purée till smooth.

Skin and bone cooled chicken breasts. Starting at wide end, slash each breast at an angle (not straight up and down) 4 or 5 times, cutting three fourths of way through. Fan breasts out into gentle curves, and arrange each fan on a bed of lettuce. Pour tofu sauce over chicken. Garnish and serve.

SERVINGS: 4. CALORIES PER SERVING: 161

Note: Dish gets its name from Japanese method of slicing foods at an angle *(usu zukuri)*.

HERBED VEGETABLE RICE

1 cup short-grain brown rice, rinsed
2 cups water
1/2 teaspoon anise seeds
2 teaspoons olive oil
2 teaspoons minced garlic
1/2 cup diced celery
1/2 cup diced red or green bell pepper
1/2 cup sliced fresh mushrooms
2 teaspoons curry powder
2 tablespoons low-sodium soy sauce
1 teaspoon grated lemon zest
Dash vegetable salt
Garnish: 1/2 cup thinly sliced scallions

Gently boil rice, water, and anise seeds in covered saucepan for 30 minutes. Set aside, still covered, for 15 minutes to allow rice to swell.

Meanwhile, prepare remaining ingredients. Heat oil in skillet and gently sauté garlic. Add celery, red or green pepper, and mushrooms. Sprinkle with curry powder and cook briefly, about 2 to 3 minutes.

Add vegetables to cooked rice and fluff mixture together.

Toss with soy sauce, lemon zest, and vegetable salt. Garnish and serve.

SERVINGS: 4 TO 8. CALORIES PER SERVING: 111 TO 222

Note: Serve as a vegetarian main course, or as a side dish with chicken, fish, or veal. Other vegetables—such as zucchini, kohlrabi, cauliflower, or broccoli—can be added.

SHRIMP SAUCE KIMINI

1 recipe Beans Niban Dashi (recipe follows)
16 medium-size shrimp, shelled, deveined, rinsed, and butterflied
1 tablespoon safflower oil (optional if grilling)
Sansho, ground ginger, or freshly ground black pepper to taste
Paprika to taste
Garnish: Lemon wedges

Spear 4 shrimp each on 4 bamboo skewers and season shrimp with pepper (or ginger) and paprika. Heat a grill or brush a cast-iron pan with oil. Quickly sauté shrimp on both sides. Cook, covered, 5 minutes, till done. To serve with the beans, arrange skewered shrimp over cooked and sauced beans on platter. Spoon some of the sauce from beans over shrimp. Garnish with the scallions from the bean recipe and lemon wedges and serve immediately.

SERVINGS: 4. CALORIES PER SERVING: 174

BEANS NIBAN DASHI

12 ounces Japanese beans or green beans, cut lengthwise
2 cups water
4 ounces tofu
2 tablespoons mirin (sweet sake)
2 tablespoons low-sodium soy sauce

1 teaspoon coarsely chopped fresh ginger
1 teaspoon coarsely chopped garlic
1 strip lemon zest (1/2 inch wide, 2 1/2 inches long)
2 teaspoons miso paste
3/4 cup vegetable broth reserved from beans, or
    Vegetable Stock (page 7), heated
2 teaspoons arrowroot
Garnish: 1/2 cup chopped scallions or 2 tablespoons
    freshly toasted sesame seeds

Steam beans in the water in covered pan 5 to 7 minutes, till done but still crisp. Drain, reserving 3/4 cup broth.

Combine broth with tofu, mirin, soy sauce, ginger, garlic, lemon zest, and miso paste in blender; blend until smooth. Add arrowroot and blend again. Pour over beans in saucepan and bring to simmer to thicken sauce. Garnish beans and serve.

SERVINGS: 4. CALORIES PER SERVING: 103

IRISH PIE

3 medium-size potatoes, peeled and cut in large chunks
2 large leeks, trimmed, thoroughly cleaned, and cut in
    large chunks
1 medium-size onion, cut in large chunks
2 teaspoons dried thyme
1/2 teaspoon sea salt
6 cups water (or as needed)
2 tablespoons corn-oil margarine
1/2 cup chopped fresh parsley
1/8 teaspoon freshly ground white pepper
1/2 cup whole-wheat bread crumbs

Preheat oven to 350 degrees.

Place potatoes, leeks, onion, thyme, and salt in heavy saucepan; add about 6 cups of water, or enough to nearly cover the vegetables. Simmer, covered, 30 minutes, or till vegetables are tender. Remove cover and cook over high heat approximately 15 minutes, or till most of liquid has evaporated. Mixture will thicken, and will require frequent stirring. Remove from heat. Add margarine, parsley, and pepper; mash with a potato masher to combine. Mixture need not be really smooth.

Grease a 7- × 11-inch baking pan with margarine. Pour potato mixture into pan and sprinkle bread crumbs over top. Bake 15 to 20 minutes, or till bubbling hot.

SERVINGS: 4 TO 8. CALORIES PER PORTION: 70 TO 140

GREEK MEATBALLS

2 tablespoons bran cereal flakes
3 tablespoons dried and crumbled whole-wheat bread
1 tablespoon whole-wheat flour
1/2 cup plain low-fat yogurt
12 ounces ground lamb
2 tablespoons chopped fresh mint
1 large fresh, ripe tomato, peeled, seeded and chopped
1 tablespoon freshly grated Parmesan or Romano cheese
1/4 cup chopped scallions
1 1/2 cups cooked, drained, and chopped fresh spinach
1 teaspoon minced garlic
Garnish: 1 large fresh, ripe tomato (diced) and chopped
    fresh parsley

Preheat broiler; or preheat oven to 375 degrees.

Mix bran, bread crumbs, flour, and yogurt. Let stand 5 minutes. Add lamb, mint, tomato, cheese, and scallions. Mix well to combine. Form 1-inch meatballs and place in heavy skillet with flame- or heatproof handle. Broil meatballs (several inches from source of heat) 10 to 15 minutes, till brown; or bake 15 minutes in center of preheated oven.

Cut off spinach stems and wash leaves thoroughly. Shake to remove excess water. Sauté garlic in nonstick pan till tender. Add spinach with remaining water clinging to leaves and cook over low heat till leaves are wilted, about 5 minutes. Transfer to platter. Serve meatballs on top of spinach; pour over excess juice from meat. Garnish and serve.

SERVINGS: 4 TO 8. CALORIES PER SERVING: 135 TO 270

GLAZED PINEAPPLE

3 cups cubed fresh pineapple
2 tablespoons brown sugar, firmly packed
3 tablespoons dark rum

Mix pineapple and brown sugar in medium-size bowl and leave at room temperature 30 minutes. Then mix thoroughly with rum and spoon into 4 dessert glasses. Refrigerate till serving time.

SERVINGS: 4. CALORIES PER SERVING: 100

BANANA ICE CREAM

4 small ripe bananas
Fresh lemon juice
1 teaspoon vanilla extract
1/2 cup low-fat milk
Garnish: Strawberries, kiwi slices, or other fresh fruit

Peel bananas, cut off tips and brown spots, and remove strings. Squeeze lemon juice over bananas. Wrap in plastic bag and freeze till solid. Meanwhile, chill 4 champagne glasses or bowls.

Near serving time, cut bananas into small pieces. Blend in food processor with vanilla extract and milk till very

smooth. If mixture becomes too thick, add more milk. Pour
into chilled glasses or bowls. Return to freezer for no longer
than 2 hours. Garnish and serve.

SERVINGS: 4. CALORIES PER SERVING: 95

Note: 12 large, fresh strawberries may be added, to give
this ice cream dessert a pink color.

HOT BANANAS AND BLUEBERRIES

4 ripe bananas
1/3 cup unfiltered apple juice
1/2 cup fresh blueberries
1 tablespoon Cointreau, Grand Marnier, or other orange
    liqueur
Garnish: Mint sprigs, strawberries, or kiwi slices

Place bananas in skillet with apple juice. Simmer gently,
covered, 4 to 5 minutes, till bananas start to soften. Turn
bananas over. Cook, uncovered, 3 to 4 minutes more, to
reduce liquid by half. Add berries; remove from heat. Add
liqueur. Shake pan to roll bananas in liquid. Garnish and
serve immediately, with the juices.

SERVINGS: 4 TO 8. CALORIES PER SERVING: 60 TO 120

Note: Two teaspoons chopped candied ginger can be substituted for the blueberries.

The Spa at Palm-Aire

When it opened in 1971, the Spa at Palm-Aire was primarily a place to be pampered while losing weight, offering facials, massages, manicures, and pedicures. Since then it has evolved into much more. The emphasis has shifted from the "fat farm" image to a total "wellness" outlook; guests at the Spa learn to incorporate healthful programs of diet and exercise into their daily routines.

This is not to say that the Palm-Aire experience is a grim, serious business; a week spent at the Spa is a week of refreshing renewal in luxurious surroundings. The Spa is part of the World of Palm-Aire, a 1,500-acre resort complex in Pompano Beach, Florida, located twenty minutes away from the Fort Lauderdale/Hollywood International Airport. Guests stay in one of the 130 deluxe rooms at the Palm-Aire Spa Hotel, surrounded by five eighteen-hole golf courses, lighted tennis and racquetball courts, and an Olympic-size pool. Or, they may be housed in one of the seventeen executive suites at the Renaissance Club, overlooking the Palm's golf course. Conference rooms and hospitality suites are also available. Beaches, shopping, and even racetracks are only minutes away; and for those guests not yet addicted to fitness, there is a cocktail lounge and a dining room that serves Continental cuisine.

But the main attraction at the World of Palm-Aire is the Spa, internationally acclaimed, visited by such celebrities as Paul Newman and Joanne Woodward, Gloria Steinem, and Carl Bernstein. Two corner rooms on the top floor of the Spa Hotel have been made into the Elizabeth Taylor Suite, in honor of her visits to the resort.

A visit to the Spa begins with a doctor's examination and an interview by a personal fitness counselor to ascertain each guest's abilities and goals. This evaluation is the basis for the Exercise Prescription, the central element of the Palm-Aire plan. The guests meet with their fitness counselor again in midweek to check their progress and, if necessary, change their program. At the end of the week the counselor reviews the individualized program once more and fashions a workable, at-home Exercise Prescription for each guest.

While weight reduction and control is not the most prevalent concern of guests at the Spa, it is an important part of the total wellness concept.

A visit to the Spa at Palm-Aire begins with low-calorie drinks, vegetable hors d'oeuvres, and dinner on the day of arrival, and ends with lunch on the day of departure. Guests select their own food combinations from menus listing the calorie content of each item. Breakfast begins with a multiple vitamin and one choice from each of the following: juice or fruit; protein (egg, cottage cheese, or milk); starch (cereal, toast, bagel thins, or Palm-Aire bran muffins).

BRAN MUFFINS

1/2 cup whole-wheat flour
1/2 cup unprocessed bran
2 tablespoons baking powder

1/4 cup finely diced apple
1/2 cup boiling water
1 teaspoon ground cinnamon
1/2 teaspoon freshly grated nutmeg
1 egg, beaten
1 tablespoon safflower oil
1/4 cup blackstrap molasses
1/4 cup honey
3/4 cup skim buttermilk

Preheat oven to 325 degrees.

Combine flour, bran, and baking powder. In a separate bowl combine diced apple, cinnamon, nutmeg, and boiling water; place in refrigerator to cool. Combine beaten egg, oil, molasses, honey, and buttermilk; pour, along with cooled apple mixture, over dry flour mixture. Gently fold mixture till all ingredients are combined. Divide batter evenly among the cups in a 12-cup nonstick muffin tin. Bake for 35 minutes.

MAKES 12 MUFFINS. CALORIES PER MUFFIN: 75

The choice of beverage is easy; guests may have either rose-hip tea or decaffeinated coffee and, of course, water, which guests are encouraged to drink in great quantity—two quarts a day.

After breakfast, which is served from 7:30 to 9:30 A.M., a typical day might include a brisk two-and-a-half mile walk around the resort's grounds and/or one or two of the exercise classes in the gym or swimming pool, followed by a relaxing twenty-minute body wrap of linen sheets soaked in hot herbal solutions—mint, eucalyptus, camomile.

Noon to 2:00 P.M. is set aside for lunch and relaxing; there are daily luncheon lectures on health-related subjects. Lunch consists of an appetizer, usually soup or salad with low-calorie dressing, and an entrée such as Fettucine Marco, Vegetable Lasagne, Seafood Creole a la Pomme, or Stuffed Green Peppers with Jarlsberg Cheese.

DILL DRESSING

3 cups plain low-fat yogurt
1 1/2 teaspoons freshly ground black pepper
1 1/2 teaspoons garlic powder
Dash Tabasco
Dash Worcestershire sauce (optional)
1/2 cup chopped fresh dill

Place yogurt in mixing bowl and add seasonings. Mix well
with whisk. Delicious over salads and seafood.
    MAKES ABOUT 3 1/2 CUPS. CALORIES PER TABLESPOON: 10

CUCUMBER DRESSING

3 cups plain low-fat yogurt
1 1/2 teaspoons freshly ground black pepper
1 1/2 teaspoons garlic powder
Dash Tabasco
1 medium-size cucumber, peeled if desired

Place yogurt and seasonings in mixing bowl and purée cucumber in food processor. Add to yogurt and mix well with
whisk. Delicious over salads and seafood.
    MAKES ABOUT 4 CUPS. CALORIES PER TABLESPOON: 13

FETTUCINE MARCO

12 ounces fettucine
4 ounces part-skim ricotta cheese
4 egg whites
1 cup plain low-fat yogurt
4 tablespoons freshly grated Parmesan cheese
Garnish: 4 fresh parsley sprigs

Preheat oven to 325 degrees.

Cook fettucine in large saucepan of boiling water for 10 to 12 minutes. Drain noodles and run cold water over them.

Beat ricotta cheese, egg whites, and yogurt together till smooth; fold into fettucine. Turn mixture into casserole dish and bake for 15 minutes. To serve, cut noodle mixture into four equal portions, sprinkle 1 tablespoon of grated Parmesan cheese on top of each serving and garnish.

SERVINGS: 4. CALORIES PER SERVING: 185

VEGETABLE LASAGNE

8 ounces lasagne noodles
Vegetable oil
1 cup diced onion
1 cup diced green bell pepper
1 cup sliced fresh mushrooms
1 cup Palm-Aire Tomato Sauce (recipe follows)
1 cup cauliflower florets, steamed
1 cup broccoli florets, steamed
1 cup diced zucchini, steamed
1 cup diced summer squash, steamed
4 ounces part-skim ricotta cheese
2 ounces part-skim mozzarella cheese, sliced

Cook lasagne noodles in large saucepan of boiling water with a splash of vegetable oil to prevent sticking till al dente. Drain well.

Spray bottom of a saucepan with low-fat vegetable coating; add onion, green pepper, and mushrooms and sauté over low heat till tender. Add tomato sauce and let simmer, uncovered, for 10 minutes.

Preheat oven to 425 degrees.

Spray a 6-inch square baking pan lightly with low-fat vegetable oil. Line bottom of pan with half the lasagne noodles. Arrange steamed vegetables evenly over noodles and then pour tomato sauce mixture over them. Evenly distribute ricotta cheese over tomato and vegetable mixture. Place remaining lasagne noodles on top of ricotta; cover with the mozzarella. Bake for 1 hour.

To serve, cut into four 3 × 3-inch squares.

SERVINGS: 4. CALORIES PER SERVING: 200

PALM-AIRE TOMATO SAUCE

6 large fresh, ripe tomatoes
1/2 cup low-sodium tomato juice
1 1/2 teaspoons dried oregano
1 1/2 teaspoons dried basil
1 potato, wrapped in cheesecloth

Purée tomatoes in blender. Add tomato juice and herbs; blend to mix thoroughly. Remove purée to a small saucepan along with wrapped-up potato. Let sauce cook, uncovered, for 1 hour over a medium flame.

MAKES ABOUT 8 CUPS. CALORIES PER OUNCE: 10

Note: The wrapped potato is necessary to absorb the acidity out of the sauce.

SEAFOOD CREOLE A LA POMME

4 medium-size baking potatoes
1/2 cup chopped green bell pepper
1/2 cup chopped onion
1/2 cup chopped fresh mushrooms
4 ounces scallops
4 ounces shrimp, shelled, deveined, and rinsed
4 ounces Jarlsberg cheese, shredded
1 cup Palm-Aire Tomato Sauce (see preceding recipe)

Preheat oven to 425 degrees.

Bake potatoes for 50 minutes. Remove from oven, leaving oven on at 425 degrees. Slice off and discard a long strip from top of each potato. Scoop out flesh from each potato without piercing the skin. Set skins aside. Spray a skillet with low-fat vegetable coating; add green pepper, onion, and mushrooms and sauté until tender. Set aside. Place 1 ounce of shrimp and 1 ounce of scallops in each potato shell along with 1/4 cup tomato sauce. Bake for 10 minutes, then sprinkle top of each potato with 1 ounce of shredded Jarlsberg. Return potatoes to oven till cheese melts. Serve immediately, with sautéed vegetables as a side dish.

SERVINGS: 4. CALORIES PER SERVING: 220

STUFFED GREEN PEPPERS WITH JARLSBERG CHEESE

2 green bell peppers
1/2 cup sliced mushrooms
1/2 cup chopped onion
1 cup Palm-Aire Tomato Sauce (see page 26)
2 cups steamed rice
4 ounces Jarlsberg cheese
Garnish: 4 fresh parsley sprigs

Halve green peppers lengthwise and remove seeds. Steam for 5 minutes. Remove from steamer and run under cold water.

Preheat oven to 350 degrees.

Spray saucepan lightly with low-fat vegetable coating; add mushrooms and onion and sauté till tender. Add tomato sauce, along with steamed rice. Simmer for 5 minutes, stirring occasionally.

Fill each pepper half with one fourth of rice and vegetable

mixture and sprinkle with 1 ounce of Jarlsberg cheese. Place in baking dish and bake for 5 minutes. Garnish and serve immediately.

SERVINGS: 4. CALORIES PER SERVING: 170

In the afternoon guests might play golf, jog around the parcourse, or go back to the pool or gym. Interspersed with all this activity are the "pampering services," the whirlpools and Swiss showers, facials and loofa baths, and daily body massages. Guests have unlimited use of the sauna, steam room, pools (both the outdoor Olympic-size pool and the indoor hot and cold contrast pools), and exercise equipment. The Spa also furnishes exercise uniforms, except swim suits, and allows nude sunbathing in its solarium. There are separate, but equal, facilities and programs for men and women in the Spa building.

Dinner is served between 6:00 and 8:00 P.M. and features such delicacies as Stuffed Mushrooms, Lobster Pernod, Tenderloin Kabobs, Shrimp Rockefeller or Veal Parmesan.

STUFFED MUSHROOMS

8 large, fresh mushroom caps
1/2 medium-size onion
1/2 slice whole-wheat bread
1 celery stalk, trimmed and cut up
1/2 cup skim milk
4 ounces crabmeat, cooked
2 teaspoons herb seasoning

Preheat oven to 350 degrees.

Purée all ingredients except mushroom caps in food processor or blender. Stuff mushroom caps evenly with mixture. Bake mushrooms for 15 minutes. Serve immediately.

SERVINGS: 4. CALORIES PER SERVING: 75

LOBSTER PERNOD

4 lobster tails with shell (6 ounces each)
4 tablespoons skim milk
2 tablespoons Pernod liqueur

Preheat oven to 350 degrees.
    Remove lobster tail meat from shells. Slice each tail in half and drape meat over shells. Moisten each tail with 1 tablespoon of skim milk. Place tails in a small roasting pan partially filled with water. Place Pernod in an atomizer and spray over all 4 tails. Cover roasting pan with aluminum foil and bake for 8 to 10 minutes.
    SERVINGS: 4. CALORIES PER SERVING: 230

TENDERLOIN KABOBS

1 cup Palm-Aire Tomato Sauce (page 26)
1/4 cup tarragon vinegar
1 tablespoon granulated garlic
1 teaspoon chopped fresh dill
12 ounces boneless beef tenderloin
12 mushroom caps
12 cherry tomatoes
12 slices green bell pepper (2 whole peppers)
12 slices onion

Slice tenderloin into twelve 1-ounce chunks. Combine tomato sauce, vinegar, garlic, and dill in a medium-size bowl and stir. Add tenderloin chunks to marinade and let stand for 1 hour.
    Preheat broiler. Have ready 4 long metal skewers.
    Place 1 mushroom cap, 1 cherry tomato, 1 slice of green pepper, 1 slice of onion, and 1 chunk of tenderloin on one

skewer. Repeat this sequence three more times, then repeat procedure with remaining skewers. Place under broiler for 10 to 12 minutes, depending on desired doneness.

Remove food from skewers and serve.

SERVINGS: 4. CALORIES PER SERVING: 190

SHRIMP ROCKEFELLER

2 cups chopped steamed spinach
1/4 cup chopped onion
1 1/2 teaspoons Pernod liqueur
12 ounces shrimp, shelled, deveined, and rinsed
1/2 cup Mornay Sauce (recipe follows)

Place chopped spinach in strainer and rinse with running water. After draining, place spinach in a saucepan lightly sprayed with low-fat vegetable coating. Sauté spinach for 2 minutes, then add onion and Pernod. Let simmer, uncovered, over low heat for 5 minutes.

While spinach and onion mixture is simmering, steam shrimp for 3 minutes. To serve, divide spinach among 4 plates. Arrange shrimp over spinach and then top each portion with 2 tablespoons of Mornay sauce.

SERVINGS: 4. CALORIES PER SERVING: 210

MORNAY SAUCE

1 cup Chablis
2 tablespoons arrowroot
1 cup skim milk
2 ounces Jarlsberg cheese, shredded
2 teaspoons vegetable salt

Heat wine slightly in saucepan. Add arrowroot slowly, stirring constantly with small whisk till fully dissolved. Continue to stir while blending in skim milk, cheese, and vegetable salt.

MAKES ABOUT 2 1/2 CUPS. CALORIES PER OUNCE: 10

VEAL PARMESAN

4 veal leg cutlets (3 ounces each)
4 ounces part-skim mozzarella cheese
1 cup Palm-Aire Tomato Sauce (page 26)

Preheat oven to 350 degrees. Using a meat mallet, pound veal into thin scallops. Slice mozzarella cheese into four equal slices. Spray a skillet with low-fat vegetable coating, then sauté veal quickly on both sides. Remove veal to a baking pan; cover each with one slice of mozzarella. Bake until cheese melts.

Meanwhile, heat tomato sauce in a small saucepan. Remove veal from oven, top each scallop with 1/4 cup tomato sauce, and serve.

SERVINGS: 4. CALORIES PER SERVING: 220

Desserts, in keeping with Adriance's approach, are easily prepared and eye-appealing.

FRUITED YOGURT

1/2 cup plain low-fat yogurt
2 packets low-calorie sweetener
1 wedge canteloupe

Combine yogurt in mixing bowl with low-calorie sweetener. Chop up canteloupe into small pieces, add to yogurt base, and let marinate for 1 hour.

SERVINGS: 1. CALORIES: 10

APPLE-PRUNE DELIGHT

2 egg whites
1/2 teaspoon cream of tartar
1 cup Nutri-Sweet–flavored prepared whipped topping
1 small prune, pitted and finely diced
1/2 small apple, cored and finely diced
1/2 teaspoon ground cinnamon
Pinch freshly grated nutmeg

Combine egg whites with cream of tartar and beat with electric mixer till stiff peaks form. Set aside. In a small bowl place prepared whipped topping, chopped prune and apple, cinnamon, and nutmeg. Mix well. Fold in whipped egg whites. Divide equally among 6 dessert dishes. Refrigerate 2 hours prior to serving.
   SERVINGS: 6. CALORIES PER SERVING: 60

A seven-day minimum stay, called the Seven-Day Renaissance Program, is required from mid-December to mid-April, but guests during the off-season can request a shorter, four-day program. There is also a one-day so-called Commuter Program, available from May through October, that includes three exercise classes, a massage, an herbal wrap, a facial, and the use of Spa attire and facilities.

   Because the Spa at Palm-Aire educates its guests in total wellness—fitness of body, mind, and soul—it is a favorite of not only celebrities but also other busy, highly stressed individuals looking for a way to achieve and maintain a healthy lifestyle. Many corporations finance a week's stay for their executives, realizing that it is money well spent—that through improved nutrition and physical conditioning their people can achieve higher productivity. The Spa at Palm-Aire program is truly "seven days that can change your life."

Pritikin Longevity Center

Technically, the Pritikin Longevity Center of Santa Monica, California, is not a spa. It's a school—a school with a curriculum that educates its pupils in a new way of life. Founded in 1976, the Center is now housed in a full-service luxury hotel with a large ocean-view dining room and a private beach. Guest accommodations include 120 attractive rooms with private baths, telephones, color TVs, and daily maid service. There are laundry facilities on the premises, a sports store carrying exercise equipment and clothing, and a sky-lighted, 4,800-square-foot gymnasium with weight-lifting equipment and over sixty motorized treadmills and exercise bicycles. Guest services such as airport pickup, shopping trips to nearby Beverly Hills, and sightseeing excursions can be arranged; the Center is close to golf courses, tennis courts, and bowling alleys.

Both healthy people who want to know more about the Pritikin way of life and men and women with severe degenerative diseases come to the Pritikin Longevity Center. "Pritikin living" is especially beneficial to patients with heart disease, diabetes, hypertension, gout, or claudication (poor circulation to the arms and legs). Some want help in reducing risk factors such as smoking, overeating, indulgence in alcohol, or stress.

Basically, the Center has two programs, one for residents and one for outpatients. The residential program may be attended for either thirteen or twenty-six days. All insulin-dependent diabetics and overweight people with severe health problems must attend the twenty-six-day program. Others, including diabetics on oral medication, may apply for either thirteen or twenty-six days. Each applicant's current medical records are reviewed by the Center's staff of eight physicians before acceptance. The outpatient program meets three times a week for four weeks.

Both programs consist of education, exercise, and diet. Lectures on the composition of foods, the control of blood pressure, and the consequences of excess eating, with catchy titles like "Eat, Drink, and Be Wary," are part of the education courses and small group-counseling sessions designed to incorporate the Pritikin plan into a busy, daily routine after "graduation."

Participants in the program learn how to shop for the right foods, how to "order Pritikin" in restaurants, how to say no to unhealthy foods, and how to get back on the Pritikin track after occasionally (and very humanly) "cheating" a bit. A monthly newsletter, *The Center Post,* is mailed to all graduates. It contains hints about good "Pritikin legal" restaurants and stores, recipes, and articles on subjects like "how to keep children away from C.A.N.D.Y. (Continuously Advertised Nutritionally Deficient Yummies)." *The Center Post* also lists "alumni contacts" every other month so graduates can get in touch with one another. The Center's alumni include men and women from all parts of the United

States and Canada, and some from as far away as France, England, Australia, South Africa, and India.

New arrivals at the Longevity Center are given a complete physical examination, including a treadmill tolerance test to determine their daily "exercise prescription." Additional appointments with a physician are scheduled twice a week to evaluate progress. Participants are then assigned to a daily, one-hour exercise class with ten or twelve other guests of equal endurance levels. Classes are noncompetitive and strictly supervised by physiologists.

Walking along the ocean is an important part of the exercise prescription—cardiac participants may be advised to take two twenty-minute walks per day with speed and duration increasing as fitness increases. Individuals with no illnesses may jog or attend aerobic dance or weight-lifting classes. Almost everyone can participate in at least one of the other activities offered at the Center—yoga, race walking, back exercises, and cardiopulmonary resuscitation. Graduates are given a home exercise prescription to continue to build strength and endurance and control their weight.

The Pritikin diet consists primarily of fresh and cooked fruits and vegetables, whole grains, nonfat dairy products, and small amounts of fish and poultry. Salt, sugar, alcohol, and caffeine are prohibited. Graduates of the Center on maintenance diets are permitted occasional small servings of lean meat.

Food is available six times a day in the Center's dining room. Dinner is served by waiters and waitresses; all other meals and snacks are buffet-style. The food is very good. Taste buds accustomed to extra salt, sugar, and fat may take a few days to adjust, but the participants soon begin to enjoy the natural flavors of their food. And, as their improved diets pay off with increased energy and a greater feeling of well-being, the benefits of the Pritikin diet plan soon become evident.

MUSHROOM BARLEY SOUP

1/4 cup medium barley
1 1/2 cups chopped onion
1 1/2 cups sliced carrots
1 cup sliced celery
4 cups beef stock
3 1/4 cups sliced fresh mushrooms
1/4 cup dry white wine
1 tablespoon low-sodium soy sauce
1 clove garlic, minced

Combine barley, onion, carrots, celery, and beef stock in a saucepan and cook, covered, 20 minutes. Add mushrooms and wine, re-cover, and cook 10 minutes longer. Add garlic and soy sauce. Cook another 5 to 10 minutes, till barley is tender, then serve.

SERVINGS: 6. CALORIES PER SERVING: 54

NAVY BEAN SOUP

1 1/4 cups dried navy beans
1 bay leaf
8 cups defatted chicken stock (or as needed)
1 clove garlic, peeled
1/4 cup sliced leeks
3/4 cup peeled, seeded, and diced tomatoes
3/4 cup chopped onion
3/4 cup chopped celery
1 package (10 ounces) frozen cut green beans
1/2 cup peeled, chopped potato
1/4 teaspoon dried dillweed
1/4 teaspoon garlic powder
1/4 teaspoon onion powder

1/4 teaspoon dried thyme
1/4 teaspoon dried basil
1/4 teaspoon dry mustard

Put navy beans, bay leaf, and 8 cups stock in a 5-quart saucepan. Simmer, covered, till beans are tender but still firm, about 1 hour. Remove bay leaf. Purée one third of the beans with the garlic.

Put puréed beans back into saucepan along with rest of vegetables and the seasonings. Simmer, covered, till vegetables are tender, about 45 minutes. Add more stock if necessary.

SERVINGS: 10. CALORIES PER SERVING: 74

CELERY ROOT SALAD

2 cups diced cooked celery root (see note below)
2 cups chopped cooked (canned or frozen) artichoke
    hearts
1/2 cup chopped scallions
1/2 cup chopped fresh parsley
1/3 cup red wine vinegar
1 tablespoon salt-free Dijon mustard
1 tablespoon Italian seasoning

Combine celery root, artichoke hearts, scallions, and parsley in a large bowl. In a smaller bowl mix vinegar and mustard. Pour vinegar/mustard mixture over vegetables, sprinkle with Italian seasoning, and toss. Refrigerate for several hours or overnight.

SERVINGS: 8. CALORIES PER SERVING: 28

Note: If using fresh celery root, steam and peel before you dice. If you use canned (look for it in gourmet and foreign food sections; it's imported from Germany), be sure to rinse well to remove the salt solution before dicing.

ASPARAGUS PUDDING

3/4 pound fresh asparagus, trimmed and diced
1 package (10 ounces) frozen green peas
4 slices whole-wheat bread
3/4 cup nonfat milk
1/2 teaspoon onion powder
1/2 teaspoon garlic powder
1 teaspoon low-sodium soy sauce
4 egg whites, beaten to soft peaks

Steam asparagus 5 minutes. Add peas and steam 5 minutes longer.
Preheat oven to 375 degrees.
    Soak bread in milk. After bread has absorbed milk, put into a food processor and blend till smooth. Add asparagus and process for 1 to 2 seconds to blend. Add drained peas and seasonings. Process for 1 to 2 seconds longer to blend. Remove to bowl; fold in beaten egg whites. Pour mixture into a 9-inch square nonstick baking pan or into individual soufflé dishes. Bake for 45 minutes for the baking dish and 30 to 35 minutes for the individual soufflés. Serve immediately.
    SERVINGS: 4. CALORIES PER SERVING: 132

MOROCCAN VEGETABLES

4 medium-size sweet potatoes, peeled and cut in 1/2-inch
    dice (about 4 cups)
2 large onions, cut in 1/2-inch dice (about 2 cups)
3 cups cooked garbanzo beans
1 cup chicken stock
1/2 cup diced (1/2 inch) red bell pepper
1/2 cup diced (1/2 inch) green bell pepper

3 cups sliced zucchini
2 large fresh, ripe tomatoes, seeded and cut in 1/2-inch dice

Sauce
1 tablespoon lemon juice
1/2 teaspoon ground cumin
1/2 teaspoon ground red (cayenne) pepper
1/2 teaspoon garlic powder
1/4 teaspoon saffron
1/2 teaspoon ground coriander
3/4 teaspoon ground cinnamon

Combine sweet potatoes, onions, garbanzos, and chicken stock in a large saucepan. Bring stock to a boil, then reduce heat and simmer, covered, for 20 minutes, or till onions and potatoes are almost tender. Add remaining vegetables and cook, covered, 10 minutes. Uncover and cook 10 minutes longer. Meanwhile, combine sauce ingredients in a small saucepan and heat till the spices dissolve. Mixture will look like a paste. Add to cooked vegetables; cook, uncovered, for 5 minutes. Serve as is, or over brown rice.

SERVINGS: 8. CALORIES PER SERVING: 200

Note: If there is too much liquid when serving vegetables alone, drain off 1 cup and save it to be used in soups or other sauces. Do not drain if vegetables are served over brown rice.

CHILAQUILES

1 can (10 ounces) Rosarita Enchilada Sauce
1 can (15 ounces) salt-free tomato sauce
6 corn tortillas, cut in strips
1/2 cup canned, diced, peeled green chilies
1 package (10 ounces) frozen corn or other vegetable of
    your choice
1/4 teaspoon garlic powder
Garnish: Chopped scallions

Combine all ingredients except scallions in a large skillet or
saucepan. Cook gently till vegetables are cooked and tortillas
are soft, but not mushy; about 10 minutes. Garnish and
serve.
     SERVINGS: 6. CALORIES PER SERVING: 125

PASTA FAGIOLI

1 cup dried pinto beans
3 cups defatted chicken stock (or as needed)
1 1/4 cups chopped onion
1/2 cup chopped celery
1 1/4 cups sliced carrots
2 1/2 cups diced tomatoes
1 cup diced green bell pepper
1 clove garlic, minced
1 teaspoon Italian seasoning
1/2 teaspoon dried rosemary
1/8 to 1/4 teaspoon ground red (cayenne) pepper
1/2 cup cooked macaroni

Put beans in a saucepan and cover with water. Cook, covered, till almost tender, a little over 1 hour. Drain; return to

saucepan. Add 3 cups chicken stock and onion and cook, covered, 20 minutes. Add remaining vegetables and seasonings. Cook, covered, 20 to 30 minutes or longer. Add macaroni and more broth if necessary; heat through and serve.

SERVINGS: 8. CALORIES PER SERVING: 90

CARIBBEAN STUFFED CHAYOTE SQUASH

3 chayote squash, halved, seeded, and flesh scooped out
1/2 cup chopped onion
1/2 cup peeled, seeded, and diced tomato
1/2 cup peeled, diced yam
1/2 cup diced green bell pepper
1/2 cup cooked brown rice
1/2 teaspoon garlic powder
1 tablespoon low-sodium soy sauce
1/4 teaspoon Tabasco
Garnish: 2 tablespoons finely chopped fresh parsley

Preheat oven to 350 degrees.

Steam all the vegetables together except the chayote shells. Mix steamed vegetables with the cooked rice and seasonings. Fill chayote shells with the mixture and bake, covered, for 20 minutes. Uncover and bake for 10 minutes more.

Sprinkle with chopped parsley and serve.

SERVINGS: 6. CALORIES PER SERVING: 55

POTATO BARLEY CASSEROLE (KRUPNIK)

1 1/2 cups medium barley
7 cups beef broth (or as needed)
2 cups peeled, diced potato
3 cups chopped onion
1/2 cup finely chopped celery
3 cups sliced fresh mushrooms
3 cups sliced carrots
1 tablespoon low-sodium soy sauce
1 tablespoon garlic purée

Cook barley, covered, in 3 cups of the beef broth in a saucepan about 30 minutes. In separate saucepan, cook potatoes and onions, covered, in remaining 4 cups broth for 30 minutes. Add remaining vegetables and the seasonings to potato mixture and cook, covered, 15 minutes longer, adding more broth if necessary. Stir in the cooked barley and serve.

SERVINGS: 10. CALORIES PER SERVING: 85

BLACK-EYED PEA CASSEROLE

2 cups dried black-eyed peas
6 cups chicken stock or water
4 cups chopped onion
1 tablespoon garlic purée
1 cup chopped celery
2 tablespoons tomato paste
1/2 cup water
1 can (8 ounces) green chili salsa
1 tablespoon low-sodium soy sauce
1/2 cup brown rice
1 cup water

Cook peas, covered, in stock in large saucepan over low heat till almost tender, about 45 minutes. Drain and rinse. Return to saucepan and add remaining ingredients except rice and water. Re-cover and simmer another 45 minutes.

Meanwhile, steam rice with the water for 45 minutes.

To serve, stir together rice and pea mixture or layer in a casserole dish, with rice on bottom and pea mixture on top.

SERVINGS: 8. CALORIES PER SERVING: 96

JAMAICAN FISH STEW

2 cups peeled, diced butternut squash or yams, steamed
2 cups peeled, seeded, and diced tomatoes
2 cups cooked brown rice
1 tablespoon lime juice
1 clove garlic, minced
1 tablespoon low-sodium soy sauce
1/2 cup dry white wine
3/4 pound cod fillets, cubed
1/8 teaspoon coconut extract
Garnish: 1/2 cup finely chopped scallions

Put the squash or yams, tomatoes, brown rice, lime juice, garlic, and soy sauce in a 3-quart saucepan and simmer, covered, for 20 minutes. Add wine and fish; cover and cook 15 minutes. Add coconut extract and stir to blend. Serve sprinkled with scallions.

SERVINGS: 6. CALORIES PER SERVING: 190

PRITIKIN PINEAPPLE CHICKEN

1 teaspoon grated fresh ginger
1 clove garlic, minced
1 shallot, minced
1 cup chicken stock
3/4 cup chopped onion
3/4 cup unsweetened pineapple juice
9 ounces boneless, skinless chicken breasts, cubed
3/4 cup sliced mixed red and green bell pepper
1 cup cubed fresh pineapple
1 tablespoon low-sodium soy sauce
1/4 teaspoon poultry seasoning
1/4 cup tomato purée
1 tablespoon cornstarch
1/4 cup water
1 tablespoon frozen unsweetened apple juice concentrate,
    thawed

Combine ginger, garlic, shallot, and chicken stock in a large saucepan, simmer, covered, for 10 minutes. Add onion and cook, covered, an additional 5 minutes. Add pineapple juice; simmer, covered, for 1 minute. Add chicken, peppers, pineapple, seasoning, soy sauce, and tomato purée. Simmer, covered, for 10 minutes. Dissolve the cornstarch in 1/4 cup water and apple juice concentrate; blend into chicken mixture. Cook, stirring constantly, until thickened and clear, about 1 minute more. Serve over steamed brown rice.

SERVINGS: 6. CALORIES PER SERVING: 120

BUTTONS AND BOWS

4 to 8 ounces lean flank steak, ground
1 teaspoon onion powder

1 teaspoon garlic powder
1 jar (7 1/2 ounces) spaghetti sauce
1 can (15 ounces) chili beans in chili gravy
1 tablespoon Italian seasoning
1 package (16 ounces) frozen mixed vegetables such as
    broccoli, cauliflower, and carrot medley
1 package (8 ounces) bow pasta, cooked

Brown ground meat in a nonstick skillet. Drain off all rendered fat. Add remaining ingredients except pasta and cook,
covered, for 20 minutes. Add pasta to meat/bean/vegetable
mixture and serve immediately.
    SERVINGS: 8. CALORIES PER SERVING: 233

BEEF AND RICE SKILLET

8 ounces lean flank steak, ground
2 tablespoons chicken stock
2 tablespoons dry sherry or dry white wine
1 large clove garlic, minced
1 medium-size onion, chopped
2 cups sliced fresh mushrooms
1/4 cup sliced water chestnuts
2 tablespoons chopped pimiento
2 tablespoons chopped green chilies
1 teaspoon low-sodium soy sauce
1 tablespoon salt-free Dijon mustard
1 to 2 cups hot, cooked brown rice

Brown ground meat in a nonstick skillet. Drain off all the
rendered fat. Remove and reserve meat; make sure skillet is
fat free. Add garlic, onion, sherry, and chicken stock to skillet; simmer, uncovered, till onion is tender. Add mushrooms
and cook till soft. Add the water chestnuts, pimiento, chilies,
soy sauce, mustard, and cooked, drained ground beef. Cook

until heated through, then stir in cooked brown rice and serve immediately.

SERVINGS: 2. CALORIES PER SERVING: 260

Note: Cooked millet or kasha can be substituted for the rice. Meat mixture can also be served by itself, accompanied by noodles.

CHICKEN CURRY

1 cup peeled, chopped apple
1 cup sliced celery
1/2 cup chopped onion
1 clove garlic, minced
1 1/2 cups defatted chicken stock
1 cup sliced fresh mushrooms
2/3 cup instant nonfat dry milk
2 tablespoons cornstarch
1 to 2 teaspoons curry powder
2 cups diced, cooked chicken

Combine apple, celery, onion, garlic, and 2 tablespoons of the chicken stock in a saucepan. Simmer, uncovered, till onion is translucent; add mushrooms and cook 2 minutes longer. Combine remaining chicken stock, nonfat dry milk, cornstarch, and curry powder; stir into vegetable mixture. Cook, stirring, till mixture thickens and bubbles. Add chicken and heat through. Serve with brown rice (Confetti Rice Mold) and various condiments, such as the following:
Raisins
Sliced scallions
Chopped red apple
Grated hard-cooked egg white
Chopped tomatoes

SERVINGS: 6. CALORIES PER SERVING: 141

CONFETTI RICE MOLD

1 package (10 ounces) frozen peas
4 cups hot, cooked brown rice
3 tablespoons chopped pimiento

Cook peas according to package directions. Drain. Combine with remaining ingredients and press into a 5 1/2-cup ring mold. Unmold at once on hot platter.

SERVINGS: 12. CALORIES PER SERVING: 100

JEWEL OF FRUIT PIE

1/2 cup plus 1 tablespoon Grape-Nuts cereal
2 ripe bananas
1/3 cup frozen unsweetened apple juice concentrate, thawed
1/2 cup water
2 tablespoons cornstarch
1 cup frozen pitted black cherries, partially thawed
1 cup frozen strawberries, partially thawed
1 cup frozen blueberries, partially thawed
1 apple, cored and grated

Preheat oven to 350 degrees.
   Sprinkle the 1/2 cup Grape-Nuts in a layer to evenly cover bottom of an 8-inch square nonstick baking pan. Slice bananas lengthwise and arrange over Grape-Nuts. Combine apple juice concentrate, water, and cornstarch in a saucepan. Cook, uncovered, over medium-low heat till thickened. Stir thawed fruit and grated apple into cornstarch mixture. Pour over bananas and spread evenly. Sprinkle the 1 tablespoon Grape-Nuts on top for a streusel effect. Bake for 1 hour.

Serve at room temperature or refrigerate and serve the following day.

SERVINGS: 6. CALORIES PER SERVING: 110

Note: Other unsweetened frozen fruit or fresh fruit may be substituted. A combination of fruits is best.

PRITIKIN FLAN

1/2 cup frozen unsweetened apple juice concentrate, thawed
1/2 teaspoon ground cinnamon
3 tablespoons cornstarch
1/4 cup water
2 1/2 cups milk
1/2 cup plus 1 tablespoon egg whites
1 teaspoon vanilla extract
1 teaspoon finely grated lemon zest
Optional garnish: Sliced fresh fruit

Mix 1/4 cup of the apple juice concentrate with the cinnamon in a small saucepan; heat till cinnamon dissolves. Set aside.

Blend cornstarch with water to dissolve. Combine remaining 1/4 cup apple juice concentrate, the milk, egg whites, vanilla, and lemon zest in medium-size saucepan. Add cornstarch mixture and bring to a boil, then lower heat to medium and cook, stirring constantly, till mixture is thickened.

Coat heatproof sherbet glasses with the apple juice/cinnamon syrup. Pour thickened custard into coated glasses. Let cool, then refrigerate for several hours. To serve, garnish with fresh sliced fruit, if desired.

SERVINGS: 6. CALORIES PER SERVING: 110

APPLESAUCE COOKIE CHEWS

3 egg whites
2 cups unsweetened applesauce (see note below)
1 cup frozen unsweetened apple juice concentrate, thawed
4 cups whole-wheat flour
1 teaspoon baking soda
1 teaspoon freshly grated nutmeg
1 teaspoon ground cinnamon
1/4 teaspoon ground cloves
1/2 cup Grape-Nuts cereal

Preheat oven to 400 degrees.

Beat egg whites until foamy in a bowl; stir in applesauce and apple juice concentrate. Combine flour and spices; add to applesauce mixture, then fold in Grape-Nuts. Drop batter by teaspoonfuls onto a nonstick baking sheet. Bake 8 to 10 minutes.

MAKES 7 DOZEN COOKIES. CALORIES PER COOKIE: 25

Note: Cored, peeled fresh apples, puréed in a food processor, can be substituted for the applesauce.

STRAWBERRY CHIFFON

1 pint fresh strawberries
1/2 cup frozen unsweetened apple juice concentrate, thawed
1/2 cup water
1 tablespoon unflavored gelatin
1/2 cup cold water
1 cup plain nonfat yogurt
1/4 teaspoon orange extract
1/4 teaspoon almond extract
1/4 cup egg whites, stiffly beaten
Optional garnish: 6 whole fresh strawberries and 6 fresh
      mint leaves

In a blender chop, but do not purée, strawberries. Set aside. Bring the apple juice concentrate and 1/2 cup water to a boil. Dissolve gelatin in the 1/2 cup cold water and add to the hot juice mixture. Let cool slightly, then stir in yogurt, extracts, and chopped strawberries. Chill till almost set, then fold in stiffly beaten egg whites.

Divide mixture between 6 sherbet glasses. Refrigerate for several hours.

To serve, garnish each serving with a whole strawberry and a mint leaf, if desired.

SERVINGS: 6. CALORIES PER SERVING: 90

Note: Other fruits may be substituted for the strawberries; do not, however, use pineapple, papaya, or kiwi fruit.

FRENCH APPLE TART

1 cup Grape-Nuts cereal (*not* the flakes)
1/3 cup plus 3 tablespoons frozen unsweetened apple
    juice concentrate, thawed
1/2 teaspoon ground cinnamon
3 medium-size apples, peeled, cored, and thinly sliced
2 teaspoons lemon juice
1 tablespoon cornstarch
2/3 cup water

Preheat oven to 350 degrees.

Moisten cereal with the 3 tablespoons apple juice concentrate in a 9-inch square or round nonstick baking pan; pat into a thin, even layer. Sprinkle with 1/4 teaspoon of the cinnamon. Arrange the sliced apples in rows (or, if using a round baking pan, in concentric circles), over crust, overlapping slightly. Sprinkle with lemon juice and remaining 1/4 teaspoon cinnamon.

Cover with parchment paper and then aluminum foil. Bake for 45 minutes, or till apples are tender.

Remove tart from oven and cool to room temperature. Combine the cornstarch, 1/3 cup apple juice concentrate, and water in a saucepan. Cook, stirring till mixture thickens and is clear. Spoon over tart, spreading into an even glaze with a pastry brush.

At this point you may either chill, if the tart is to be served much later, or leave at room temperature to serve.

SERVINGS: 6. CALORIES PER SERVING: 130

The International Health and Beauty Spa at Gurney's Inn

A haven for harried New Yorkers, Gurney's Inn at Montauk, Long Island, is only 115 miles from Manhattan. For those who journey to this luxurious resort-and-spa from other countries or other parts of this country, the Monte family, keepers of the inn, are happy to provide complimentary transportation to and from local airports and railroad stations and will arrange New York City trips for theatergoers, shoppers, and sightseers. Locally, in addition to the spa facilities, guests can enjoy golf, tennis, sailing, or charter boat fishing.

Gurney's Inn opened in 1926; since then it has expanded from an oceanfront resort for vacationers to a year-round luxury complex that includes time-sharing cooperative vacation units and a well-appointed conference center. The main attraction, of course, is the International Health and Beauty Spa.

The theme of the spa is the sea and its life-giving, curative powers. Nick Monte, the spa's creator, firmly believes that the world would need fewer psychiatrists if people spent more time near the ocean. With this in mind he has investigated the techniques used by European marino-therapeutic spas and has designed a cosmopolitan facility utilizing Gurney's prime location on the Atlantic seaboard to provide threefold benefits: sea air, seawater, and sea food, from oysters to seaweed.

Botticelli's Venus, copied in bronze, greets visitors as a tangible symbol of the spa's sea-renewal philosophy. After an initial medical survey, including a four-page health questionnaire and a blood pressure check, guests are free to experience the wide range of therapies offered at Gurney's.

Thalasso therapies—from the Greek word for "seawater" —include exercises and swimming in the sixty-foot, eighty-degree seawater pool, a Roman Jacuzzi bath filled with filtered ocean water, and the famous German thalasso massage. For this massage the guest is immersed in a special tub filled with filtered ocean water heated to body temperature. Gentle jets of water provide flotation while six more powerful nozzles set into the tub's sides give a deeper massage enhanced by a trained technician's skillful manipulation with yet another hose.

Other hydrotherapies include alternating hot and cold showers of both seawater and fresh water—the Scotch Hoses or Swiss showers—followed by special massages. One such massage is the Salt Glow, a mixture of almond oil and imported Dead Sea salt that is massaged into the entire body and sprayed off with fresh water.

More than a dozen different physiotherapies (exercise classes) are available at Gurney's. Guests can start the day with a solitary sunrise beach walk or, a little later, join the others for a brisk combination of walking, stretching, calisthenics, and jogging along the shore. Weather permitting, many of the exercise classes are held outside to give guests the added advantages of the ocean's revitalizing power—the beneficial negative ions of the sea air and the calming sounds of the surf.

The programs at the resort include the spa cuisine, the health questionnaire, use of spa facilities, and evening lectures on various subjects. Five resident plans are available— the Seven-Day Rejuvenating Plan, the Executive Longevity Programme, the Four-Day Mid-Week Plan, the European Cellulite Control Programme, and a Day of Beauty/Vitality for women/men.

The benefits of a visit to the International Health and Beauty Spa are meant to remain with guests long after the visit ends. Guests are taught biofeedback and meditation methods of stress reduction and can attend sessions to develop and enhance their self-image.

Golfers, fishermen, sunrise watchers, and other early risers may request breakfast as early as 4:00 A.M.; the dining room officially opens at 7:30 A.M. All spa food is prepared without added salt, sugar, or fat—and fresh herbs and spices are grown in the spa's pantry garden. Menus at the spa are rotated every eight days, and calorie counts are shown for each selection. Weight-conscious guests are encouraged to adhere to 800 to 1,200 calories a day—a goal made easily attainable by the chef's use of low-calorie appetizers, dressings, stocks, and desserts.

STUFFED CHERRY TOMATOES

Remove tops of cherry tomatoes. Scoop out seeds and stuff each with a piece of crabmeat or lobster. Place on slice of zucchini or cucumber and serve with toothpick to hold it together.

CALORIES PER TOMATO: 14

DEVILED EGGS

12 eggs, hard-cooked
1/2 cup low-fat cottage cheese
2 green bell pepper slices, chopped
1 tablespoon Dijon mustard
Herb seasoning to taste
Garnish: Paprika

Peel shells from eggs, chill, and slice in half lengthwise.
Remove yolks. Mix cottage cheese, green pepper, mustard,
and herb seasoning with one of the yolks; reserve remainder
for another use. Spoon mixture into egg white halves. Sprinkle with paprika.

MAKES 24. CALORIES PER 1/2 EGG: 17

SALMON MOUSSE

1 tablespoon unflavored gelatin
1/2 cup boiling water
1 can (16 ounces) red salmon, drained
1 tablespoon lemon juice
1 cup plain low-fat yogurt
1/2 teaspoon paprika
1 teaspoon dried dillweed
1/4 teaspoon garlic powder
1/2 teaspoon freshly ground black pepper
Garnish: Salad greens, cherry tomatoes, fresh parsley
      sprigs, and lemon and/or lime wedges

Add gelatin to boiling water; stir constantly till dissolved.
Skin, bone, and mash salmon. Stir into gelatin mixture along
with lemon juice, yogurt, and seasonings and blend thoroughly. Pour into 1-quart mold. Refrigerate at least 4 hours.

Unmold onto a serving platter and surround with salad greens. Garnish with cherry tomatoes, parsley, and lemon and/or lime wedges.

SERVINGS: 8. CALORIES PER SERVING: 95

Note: May also be used as a dip with whole-wheat or rice crackers.

GAZPACHO ANDALUSIAN

2 cloves garlic (or 1/2 teaspoon garlic powder)
1 green bell pepper
1 small onion
1 cucumber
3 fresh, ripe tomatoes or 1 can (16 ounces) whole
    tomatoes, drained
2 cups salt-free tomato juice
1/4 cup wine vinegar
1/2 teaspoon dried oregano
1/2 teaspoon dried basil or two fresh leaves
1/2 teaspoon dried dillweed
1/4 teaspoon freshly ground black pepper
Dash Tabasco
Dash chili powder

Wash and/or peel and cut all vegetables into proper size for blender. Combine tomato juice, vinegar, oregano, basil, and dillweed in a saucepan; heat to simmer to bring out flavor of herbs. Remove from heat and let cool.

Stir black pepper, Tabasco, and chili powder into cooled tomato juice mixture. Blend one third of tomato juice mixture with one third of the vegetables at a time. Refrigerate blended mixture till chilled.

To serve, spoon gazpacho into 3 individual soup bowls and accompany with the following, each in a chilled bowl:

1 small onion, coarsely chopped
1 small cucumber, peeled and coarsely chopped
1/2 green bell pepper, seeded and coarsely chopped

SERVINGS: 3. CALORIES PER SERVING: 50

POTATO LEEK SOUP

1 onion, sliced
3 leeks (white parts only), thoroughly cleaned and thinly
    sliced
5 cups chicken stock
1 pound potatoes, peeled and sliced
1 stalk celery, trimmed and sliced
4 sprigs fresh parsley
1/2 teaspoon dried marjoram
1/8 teaspoon freshly ground white pepper
Garnish: Minced fresh chives

Simmer onion and leeks, covered, in 1 cup of the stock in
large saucepan for 10 minutes. Add remaining stock,
potatoes, celery, parsley, and seasonings. Bring to a boil,
then reduce heat and simmer, covered, for 20 minutes, or till
potatoes are soft. Purée in blender.

Pour into individual bowls, garnish, and serve immediately.

SERVINGS: 8. CALORIES PER SERVING: 65

ASPARAGUS SOUP

8 cups chicken stock
1 medium-size onion, chopped
1 medium-size potato, peeled and thinly sliced
1/8 teaspoon freshly ground black pepper
1/2 teaspoon dried tarragon
2 cans (14 ounces each) asparagus, drained but 1 cup
    liquid reserved
1 tablespoon chopped fresh parsley

Combine 1 cup of the chicken stock, the onion, potato, pepper, and tarragon in medium-size saucepan. Cover and simmer for 10 minutes, or till potato is tender. Cut off tips of
asparagus and save for garnish. Add asparagus and reserved
liquid to potato-onion mixture and simmer 5 minutes longer.
Remove from heat.
    Place 1 cup of the chicken stock, about one third of the
vegetable mixture, and the parsley in blender; blend at
high speed. Pour into clean saucepan and repeat procedure
twice, using 2 more cups stock and remaining vegetable
mixture. Add 1 cup stock to saucepan and simmer soup,
covered, for about 1 1/2 hours, or till it reaches desired
consistency.
    Garnish with asparagus tips to serve.
    SERVINGS: 8. CALORIES PER SERVING: 40

TABASCO SALAD DRESSING

1/2 cup plain low-fat yogurt
1 teaspoon prepared mustard
1 teaspoon minced scallions
1 teaspoon dried dillweed
2 teaspoons minced fresh parsley

1/4 teaspoon garlic powder
1/2 teaspoon minced fresh chives
2 to 3 drops Tabasco

Shake all ingredients in tightly covered pint jar till well blended. Store in refrigerator.

MAKES ABOUT 2/3 CUP. CALORIES PER TABLESPOON: 18–20

Note: A tasty dressing for mixed salad vegetables.

Variation: Eliminate Tabasco and serve with sliced cucumbers.

HERB SALAD DRESSING

1 cup water
1 teaspoon cornstarch
1 tablespoon vegetable oil
2 1/2 tablespoons vinegar
3/4 teaspoon dried parsley
3/4 teaspoon dried basil
3/4 teaspoon dried oregano
1 teaspoon dried chervil
Freshly ground white pepper to taste
Garlic powder to taste

Use enough of the water to dissolve cornstarch. Combine mixture with rest of water and remaining ingredients in a saucepan. Bring to a boil, then reduce heat and simmer for a few minutes, stirring occasionally. Let cool.

If necessary, before serving, whisk dressing for a smoother consistency.

MAKES ABOUT 1 1/4 CUPS. CALORIES PER TABLESPOON: 7

The programs at the International Health & Beauty Spa are permissive. There is no rigid planning of guests' time, but in spite of this permissiveness, some of the therapies are very rigorous, requiring the staff's encouragement and, occasionally, gentle admonishments. Rolfing, a technique of "structural integration" perfected by Dr. Ida P. Rolf, is available in a series of ten weekly sessions. These treatments forcefully move and stretch tissues, sometimes causing acute pain. Believers in Rolfing swear the results make the suffering worthwhile. Shiatsu, Japanese finger-pressure massage based on acupuncture theories, is sometimes uncomfortable, but a shiatsu session cannot be halted halfway without disturbing the harmony of mind and body. Again, the results in terms of relaxation and stress reduction are said to be worth the discomfort.

Other global therapies include Russian steam rooms, Finnish saunas, and Italian fango packs, in which tense shoulder and back muscles and stiff joints are packed in a hot mineral, paraffin, and plant part solution. Guests may also choose a Chinese reflexology foot massage, an Indian facial, or a session of Swedish massage to renew their post-exercise energy.

Lunch and dinner at Gurney's are also energy renewing, with an impressive array of healthful and delicious entrées. Popular luncheon items are:

ARMENIAN BAKED STUFFED EGGPLANT

3 small eggplants (about 1 pound each)
1 onion, chopped
4 shallots, chopped
1 clove garlic, chopped
1/2 cup stock (or as needed)
2 cups fresh mushrooms, finely chopped
1/4 cup chopped fresh parsley
1 teaspoon dried oregano
1/4 teaspoon freshly ground black pepper
1/4 teaspoon dried basil
6 ounces low-fat mozzarella cheese, shredded

Preheat oven to 400 degrees.

Wash eggplant; do not peel. Cut in half lengthwise and hollow out inside, leaving about 1/4-inch rim. Place shells in baking dish and bake till almost done, about 35 minutes; leave oven on at 400 degrees.

Finely chop insides of eggplant. Simmer onion, shallots, and garlic, uncovered, with as little stock as necessary until transparent. Add mushrooms, chopped eggplant, and seasonings; simmer, uncovered, till vegetables are tender.

Spoon eggplant and mushroom mixture into prebaked eggplant shells. Top with shredded cheese. Bake till hot throughout and cheese has melted. Place under broiler for a few minutes, if desired. Serve immediately.

SERVINGS: 6. CALORIES PER SERVING: 125

VEGETABLES AU GRATIN

2 small onions or 1 large, chopped
4 cloves garlic, minced
1/4 cup dry white wine
Freshly ground black pepper, dried basil, and dried
    oregano to taste
Chicken stock or vegetable stock
2 carrots, peeled and diced
1 bunch broccoli, broken into florets
1/2 large head cauliflower, broken into florets
1 large zucchini, diced
2 to 3 fresh, ripe tomatoes, seeded and diced
8 ounces low-fat mozzarella cheese, cut into eight 1-ounce
    slices

Sauté onion and garlic in dry pan till almost sticking. Add wine and seasonings, then add carrots and cook till almost tender. Add, in succession, broccoli, cauliflower, and zucchini. Cook each vegetable till almost tender before adding next; add stock as necessary as you cook. Remove from heat before adding tomatoes.

Preheat broiler.

Divide vegetable mixture among 8 ramekins; place one slice mozzarella on top of each portion and brown under broiler. Serve immediately.

SERVINGS: 8. CALORIES PER SERVING: 150

MANICOTTI ABRUZZI

1 pound low-fat cottage cheese or fat-free whey cheese
2 tablespoons chopped fresh parsley
2 tablespoons seasoned bread crumbs
2 egg whites
Dash freshly ground black pepper
6 large manicotti shells, cooked until al dente
3 cups tomato sauce

Preheat oven to 350 degrees.

Combine all ingredients except shells and tomato sauce and mix together till well blended. Stuff each manicotti shell with filling. Spread small amount of tomato sauce in baking pan. Place manicotti in pan. Spoon sauce over shells to cover. Bake, tightly covered, for 40 minutes; do not peek. Serve immediately.

SERVINGS: 6. CALORIES PER SERVING: 185

BROILED SCALLOPS

3 tablespoons dry white wine
1 tablespoon fresh lemon juice
3 ounces scallops

Preheat broiler.

Mix white wine and lemon juice and pour over scallops in shallow baking dish. Place under broiler till scallops are opaque or cooked to personal preference, no more than 5 minutes. Drain and serve immediately.

SERVINGS: 2. CALORIES PER SERVING: 110

PAELLA VALENCIA

1 medium-size onion, chopped
2 cloves garlic, minced
1/4 teaspoon garlic powder
1/4 teaspoon dried basil
1/8 teaspoon freshly ground black pepper
1/2 teaspoon dried oregano
1/2 teaspoon paprika
2 tablespoons chopped fresh parsley
1 cup seeded and chopped tomatoes
1 cup chicken stock
1/3 cup chopped green bell pepper
3/4 pound chicken breasts, skinned and boned, cut into
    small serving pieces
1/2 pound bay scallops
1/2 pound mussels in shells, scrubbed

Simmer onion and garlic, uncovered, in 1/4 cup chicken stock in Dutch oven till tender. Add remaining ingredients except for chicken and shellfish and simmer, uncovered, for 15 minutes.

Add chicken, scallops, and mussels to sauce in Dutch oven. Simmer, covered, for 10 minutes, or till scallops are opaque, mussels are open, and chicken is fork tender. Serve on a bed of rice.

SERVINGS: 6. CALORIES PER SERVING: 230

VEAL MARSALA

4 thin veal cutlets (4 ounces each)
Thinly sliced fresh mushrooms
Freshly ground black pepper to taste
2 tablespoons Marsala wine
Garnish: Chopped fresh parsley

Poach veal in stock or water. Simmer mushrooms with pepper in stock and wine. Serve on top of veal. Garnish with parsley.

SERVINGS: 4. CALORIES PER SERVING: 250

Variation:

VEAL PICCATA

As above, except eliminate mushrooms and use juice of 1 lemon and 1/4 cup of dry white wine instead of the Marsala wine.

SERVINGS: 4. CALORIES PER SERVING: 240

ORANGE WHIP

1 teaspoon unflavored gelatin
2 tablespoons frozen orange juice concentrate, thawed
2 tablespoons fresh orange juice
1/3 cup egg whites

Sprinkle gelatin over orange juice concentrate and orange juice in small saucepan; heat until gelatin dissolves, then let cool. Chill until gel forms (it will take a few hours). Whip egg whites till stiff peaks form. Fold whites into orange juice mixture. Spoon into 3 individual sherbet glasses.

SERVINGS: 3. CALORIES PER SERVING: 60

PINEAPPLE-LEMON WHIP

1 envelope unflavored gelatin
3/4 cup pineapple juice (from can of pineapple in its own
    juice)
1 cup juice-packed canned chunk pineapple
2 tablespoons lemon juice
3 egg whites
Garnish: 6 thin lemon slices

Sprinkle gelatin over pineapple juice in small saucepan; heat
till gelatin dissolves, then let cool. Blend cooled pineapple
juice mixture, pineapple, and lemon juice in blender till
smooth.

Beat egg whites until stiff peaks form. Gently fold egg
whites into pineapple mixture. Spoon into 6 individual sherbet glasses and garnish each with a lemon slice.

SERVINGS: 6. CALORIES PER SERVING: 50

BANANA-GRAPE MEDLEY

1 envelope unflavored gelatin
1/2 cup cold water
3 small ripe bananas
1 cup orange juice
1 cup seedless grapes, plus additional (halved) for garnish
6 tablespoons lemon juice

Sprinkle gelatin over cold water in medium-size saucepan;
heat till gelatin dissolves. Mash bananas. Add bananas, orange juice, grapes, and lemon juice to gelatin mixture and
blend thoroughly. Pour into a bowl and refrigerate till
syrupy.

Process mixture in blender or beat with electric mixer until fluffy. Pour into 6 individual sherbet glasses and refrigerate. To serve, garnish with halved grapes.

SERVINGS: 6. CALORIES PER SERVING: 50

Canyon Ranch

"Canyon Ranch introduces people to the elements needed for lifelong wellness—the ideal balance of body, mind, and spirit," says owner and founder Mel Zuckerman. And he should know.

In 1978, at the age of fifty—overweight, asthmatic, and suffering from hypertension—Zuckerman went to a spa for two weeks and stayed a month. He learned to enjoy nutritious food and to exercise effectively. He lost nearly thirty pounds and gained an insight into the precepts of wellness. He eagerly returned to his home in Tucson, where he and his wife, Enid, purchased an aging dude ranch and developed it into a state-of-the-art vacation fitness resort—Canyon Ranch.

Snuggled against the Santa Catalina mountains near Tucson lies the lush, sixty-acre coed resort dedicated to health and well-being. Sometimes called "the spa for all reasons," Canyon Ranch offers indoor and outdoor activities all day long—morning walks, fitness classes, yoga, racquetball, tennis, hiking, mountain-bike tours, swimming, and much more. The ultramodern 38,000-square-foot spa facility features airy, carpeted gymnasiums, a fully equipped weight room,

Jacuzzis, cold dips, steam, and sauna—plus complete massage, herbal wrap, skin care, and beauty departments. Horseback riding and golf are available nearby.

About 150 guests can stay at this secluded desert oasis to get in shape, lose weight, control stress, stop smoking, learn to better deal with arthritis, or simply to relax and rejuvenate.

Many Canyon Ranch guests arrive expecting to exercise a lot and eat very little. They've heard about spas—hour after hour of grueling, punishing sit-ups with dozens of other groaning overindulgers. And virtually no food.

They've heard that women dieters should consume only 800 calories a day, including juice breaks, and men a mere 1,000. They are wary. But they are soon delightfully surprised. The Canyon Ranch menu features an astounding array of salads and seafood, muffins and milkshakes—even steak! And one is not to believe the luscious desserts that can be had for as little as forty calories a serving!

All these gourmet delights are prepared with only fresh, natural ingredients—low in salt and saturated fat, high in fiber, and totally without refined flour or sugar. The secret is careful preparation and portion control—two things you can do at home using the simple recipes that follow.

BLUEBERRY SOUP

1/2 cup frozen unsweetened pineapple juice concentrate
1/2 cup water
1 teaspoon lemon juice
3 cups fresh or frozen unsweetened blueberries

Combine concentrate, water, and lemon juice in a blender. Add 2 cups of the blueberries and blend till smooth. Pour blueberry mixture over the remaining 1 cup blueberries and mix well. Serve cold.

SERVINGS: 6. CALORIES PER 1/2 CUP SERVING: 70

BORSCHT

3 large beets (each 2 1/2 inches in diameter)
3 large cloves garlic, peeled and crushed
1/2 teaspoon salt
1 tablespoon fructose
2 cups buttermilk
Optional garnish: 8 teaspoons plain low-fat yogurt and 8
    lemon slices

Scrub beets thoroughly, being careful not to break skins. Cut
off roots and all but 2 inches of tops. Place beets and crushed
garlic in saucepan. Add water to cover and bring to a boil.
Reduce heat, cover, and simmer for 20 minutes.

Remove beets and garlic from cooking liquid, reserving
1 cup of liquid to add later. Slip skins off beets and discard;
chop beets. Put beets in blender, along with reserved 1 cup
cooking liquid and all other ingredients except garnish;
blend until smooth.

Serve hot or cold, garnishing each serving with a teaspoon of yogurt and lemon slice, if desired.

SERVINGS: 8. CALORIES PER 1/2 CUP SERVING: 60

CHICKEN STOCK

2 to 4 pounds chicken bones, parts, and giblets (see note
    below)
1 to 2 carrots, scraped and chopped
1 to 2 celery stalks (without leaves), chopped
1 large onion, quartered
2 to 4 cloves garlic, halved
1 bay leaf
12 whole peppercorns
Cold water to cover

Put all ingredients in large pot with lid; bring water slowly to a boil. Reduce heat, cover, and simmer for 1 to 3 hours (cooking longer makes more flavorful stock). Cool to room temperature.

Remove chicken parts and vegetables and strain stock. Refrigerate, uncovered, overnight, or till fat has hardened on top. Remove fat and store stock in freezer in the size containers you most frequently use.

MAKES ABOUT 8 CUPS. CALORIES PER CUP: NEGLIGIBLE

Note: You can buy chicken parts from your butcher (wings, backs, necks, etc.) for stock or you can save chicken carcasses in the freezer until you're ready to make stock. Use all giblets except the liver.

VEGETABLE STOCK

1 small head cabbage, cored and chopped
4 onions, chopped
6 carrots, scraped and chopped
1 small bunch celery (without leaves), chopped
1 small bunch parsley, chopped
3 bay leaves
2 teaspoons dried marjoram
1 teaspoon salt
16 cups water

Combine all ingredients in large pot and bring to a boil. Reduce heat, cover, and simmer for 1 hour. Strain stock and refrigerate or store in freezer in size containers most frequently used.

MAKES ABOUT 3 QUARTS. CALORIES PER CUP: NEGLIGIBLE

EGG DROP SOUP

6 cups Chicken Stock (see page 69)
2 eggs, well beaten
Sodium-reduced soy sauce (optional)
Garnish: Chopped scallion tops

Bring chicken stock to a boil. Add beaten eggs, stirring constantly. Continue stirring till eggs are cooked and stringy. Add a drop or two of soy sauce, if desired; garnish each serving with a sprinkle of chopped scallion tops.

SERVINGS: 8. CALORIES PER 3/4-CUP SERVING: 20

CANYON RANCH GUACAMOLE

1 envelope unflavored gelatin
2 tablespoons cool water
1/4 cup boiling water
1 pound zucchini, steamed and chopped
Juice of 1/2 lemon
1/4 onion, chopped
1 large, fresh, ripe tomato, seeded and chopped
1 teaspoon salt
1/2 teaspoon chili powder
1/4 teaspoon ground cumin
1/4 teaspoon freshly ground black pepper
1 clove garlic or 1/4 teaspoon garlic powder
1/8 teaspoon Tabasco
1/2 cup sour cream

Soften gelatin in the cool water. Add boiling water and stir till gelatin is completely dissolved. Combine gelatin mixture with zucchini in blender and blend till completely smooth.

Add all other ingredients and blend till well mixed. Refrigerate several hours or overnight before serving.

SERVINGS: 8. CALORIES PER 1/2-CUP SERVING: 50

ARTICHOKE BOWLS WITH SHRIMP IN TARRAGON DILL SAUCE

8 whole artichokes, steamed
4 cups cooked, cleaned shrimp
2 cups diced celery
1 1/2 cups Tarragon Dill Sauce (recipe follows)

Make artichoke bowls by carefully removing chokes and prickly center from the cooked, cooled artichokes. Combine shrimp, celery, and 1 cup of the tarragon dill sauce and mix well. Divide mixture evenly among chilled hollowed-out artichoke bowls. Serve with remaining tarragon dill sauce as a dip for the artichoke leaves.

SERVINGS: 8. CALORIES PER SERVING: 200

TARRAGON DILL SAUCE

2 cups plain low-fat yogurt
2 1/2 teaspoons dried tarragon
4 teaspoons dried dillweed
1/4 teaspoon salt

Combine all ingredients and mix well. Cover tightly and store in refrigerator.

MAKES 2 CUPS. CALORIES PER 1/4 CUP: 35
Note: Always prepare this sauce a day ahead of time.

CURRIED TUNA SALAD WITH WALNUTS

2/3 cup chopped walnuts
5 heads Boston lettuce, torn into bite-size pieces (about
    10 cups)
3 1/2 cups juice-packed pineapple chunks, drained
3 cans (7 ounces each) white water-packed tuna, drained
    and flaked
3/4 cup Curry Dressing (recipe follows)

Toast chopped walnuts and set aside. Combine remaining
ingredients and mix thoroughly. Sprinkle each serving with
4 teaspoons toasted walnuts.

SERVINGS: 8. CALORIES PER 2 1/2-CUP SERVING: 200

CURRY DRESSING

1 cup plain low-fat yogurt
2 tablespoons low-calorie mayonnaise
1/2 teaspoon curry powder
1/8 teaspoon ground ginger
1/4 teaspoon salt
1/2 teaspoon fructose

Put all ingredients in blender and blend till smooth.

MAKES 1 CUP. CALORIES PER TABLESPOON: 25

MELON BOWLS WITH CURRIED CRAB

4 small, ripe cantaloupes
4 cups chopped, cooked crabmeat
1 teaspoon curry powder
1/8 teaspoon ground ginger
Garnish: Chopped scallion tops

Cut melons in half and remove seeds. Use melon baller to remove melon from rinds. Combine melon balls and all other ingredients except garnish and mix thoroughly. Divide mixture equally among 8 melon bowls and sprinkle top of each serving generously with chopped scallion tops.

SERVES 8. CALORIES PER SERVING: 190

CEVICHE

1 1/2 pounds red snapper fillets, cubed (3 cups)
1/2 cup lime juice
1/2 teaspoon salt
1/2 teaspoon freshly ground black pepper
2 cloves garlic, minced
1/4 cup red wine vinegar
1 large onion, finely chopped
2 teaspoons dried oregano, crushed
1/2 cup chopped fresh coriander (cilantro)
2 large fresh, ripe tomatoes, peeled and diced
1 can (2 ounces) chopped pimientos, undrained
1 can (4 ounces) chopped peeled green chiles, undrained

Combine raw fish, lime juice, salt, pepper, and garlic in glass baking dish. Mix thoroughly, cover, and refrigerate for 24 hours. Before serving, add all remaining ingredients and mix well. Refrigerate again till cold before serving.

SERVINGS: 14. CALORIES PER 1/2-CUP SERVING: 80

CANYON RANCH DRESSING

1/2 cup red wine vinegar
1/4 teaspoon freshly ground black pepper
3/4 teaspoon salt
2 teaspoons fructose

2 cloves garlic, minced, or 1/2 teaspoon garlic powder
1 1/2 teaspoons dried tarragon
1 teaspoon dried basil
3/4 teaspoon dried oregano
2 teaspoons Worcestershire sauce
1 tablespoon Dijon mustard
Juice of 1/2 lemon
1 cup corn or safflower oil
1 cup water

Combine all ingredients except water in jar with tight-fitting lid. Shake well. Add water and shake well again. Refrigerate.
    MAKES ABOUT 2 CUPS. CALORIES PER TABLESPOON: 17
    Note: The flavor is better if made a day before you plan to use it.

STUFFED ACORN SQUASH

3 acorn squash
2 1/4 cups Vegetable Stock (see page 70)
1/2 cup brown rice
1/4 cup wild rice
1/4 cup lentils
1/2 cup chopped celery
1/4 cup chopped fresh mushrooms
1/2 cup chopped carrots
4 shallots, chopped
1 small clove garlic, minced
1 tablespoon chopped fresh parsley
1/2 teaspoon dried sage
1/2 teaspoon dried thyme

Preheat oven to 350 F.
    Bake whole squash till tender, about 1 hour.
    While squash is baking, make stuffing. Cook brown rice,

wild rice, and lentils in 2 cups of the vegetable stock till done, about 40 minutes. Meanwhile, simmer celery, mushrooms, carrots, shallots, garlic, and parsley with remaining 1/4 cup vegetable stock in a saucepan till vegetables are tender. Combine rice mixture, vegetable mixture, and seasonings; mix thoroughly, then set aside.

Cut baked squash in half and scoop seeds out. Stuff each half with 1/2 cup of the stuffing and serve.

SERVINGS: 6. CALORIES PER SERVING: 135

Note: If you are making these ahead of time, place stuffed squash in baking dish and reheat in a 350-degree oven for 15 minutes before serving

TAMALE PIE

3 medium-size onions, finely chopped
3 cloves garlic, finely chopped
1 can (4 ounces) chopped peeled green chilies, undrained
2 cups corn kernels
2 tablespoons chili powder
1/2 teaspoon salt
1/4 teaspoon ground cumin
3/4 teaspoon dried thyme
1 teaspoon dried basil
1 teaspoon dried oregano
1 can (28 ounces) tomatoes, undrained
3 cups buttermilk
1 cup yellow cornmeal
2 eggs, beaten
1 1/2 cups (6 ounces) grated sharp cheddar cheese

Combine onions and garlic in a saucepan and cook, covered, over low heat, stirring occasionally to prevent scorching, till soft. Add chilies, corn, and all of the seasonings. Add all the juice from can of tomatoes. Dice tomatoes and add to mixture. Continue cooking over low heat for 15 minutes.

Preheat oven to 350 degrees.

Combine buttermilk and cornmeal in another pan and bring to a boil. Reduce heat and continue cooking, stirring constantly, till thickened. Add eggs and mix well. Combine vegetables and cornmeal mixture. Mix well and pour into a flat baking dish. Bake, uncovered, for 1 hour.

Sprinkle cheese over top and return to oven for 10 more minutes. Serve immediately.

SERVINGS: 12. CALORIES PER 3/4-CUP SERVING: 195

CIOPPINO

1 large onion, thinly sliced
1 cup chopped scallions
3 cloves garlic, finely chopped
1/2 cup finely chopped fresh parsley
1 green bell pepper, seeded and diced
3 cups tomato sauce
1 cup dry white wine
1 cup water
1/4 teaspoon dried thyme
1/4 teaspoon dried rosemary
1 teaspoon salt
1/4 teaspoon freshly ground black pepper
1 bay leaf
1 pound crabmeat, flaked, or firm white fish, cubed
1 pound shrimp, shelled, deveined, and rinsed
16 scallops or clams, in shells

Combine onion and garlic in a large saucepan and cook, covered, over low heat till soft, stirring frequently to prevent scorching. Add all remaining ingredients except seafood and mix well. Continue to simmer, covered, for 1 hour.

Add all the seafood to saucepan and continue to cook, covered, for 8 to 10 minutes, or till scallops are opaque or clams are open.

SERVINGS: 8. CALORIES PER 1 1/2-CUP SERVING: 210

BARBECUED CHICKEN

8 chicken legs
Garlic powder
2 cups Barbecue Sauce (recipe follows)

Preheat oven to 350 degrees.

Place chicken legs in baking dish and sprinkle lightly with garlic powder. Cover baking dish with lid or aluminum foil and bake for 30 minutes.

Remove baking dish from oven; cool chicken legs till they can be handled easily. Remove and discard skin and place chicken legs back in dish. Pour 1/4 cup of sauce over each chicken leg. Cover and bake for 20 more minutes.

SERVINGS: 8. CALORIES PER SERVING: 135

BARBECUE SAUCE

1 large onion, minced
1 cup tomato sauce
1/4 cup lemon juice
3 tablespoons Worcestershire sauce
2 tablespoons distilled white vinegar
2 tablespoons fructose
1 1/2 teaspoons dry mustard
1/4 teaspoon salt
1 cup water
1/2 teaspoon liquid smoke (see note on page 79)

Sauté onions, without fat, in nonstick saucepan till soft, stirring frequently to prevent scorching. Combine tomato sauce, lemon juice, Worcestershire sauce, and vinegar; add fructose, dry mustard, and salt and mix thoroughly. Add to onions in pan, along with 1 cup water. Mix well and slowly bring to a boil. Reduce heat, cover, and simmer for 30 minutes.

Remove saucepan from heat and stir in liquid smoke. Use immediately or cool to room temperature and store, covered, in refrigerator.

MAKES 2 CUPS. CALORIES PER 1/4 CUP: 25

Note: Liquid smoke (condensed hickory smoke) is available in the spice section of most supermarkets.

COLD POACHED SALMON IN DILLED CUCUMBER SAUCE

6 cups water
1 celery stalk (without leaves), sliced
1 carrot, sliced
1 onion, chopped
1 lemon, sliced
2 tablespoons distilled white vinegar
2 pounds salmon steaks
2 cups Tarragon Dill Sauce (page 72)
1 large cucumber, peeled and grated

Combine water, celery, carrot, onion, lemon slices, and vinegar in a saucepan and bring to a boil. Reduce to a simmer and continue cooking for at least 30 minutes.

Wrap salmon in cheesecloth and place in simmering stock. Cook till salmon is opaque, about 8 minutes. Lift salmon out of liquid and remove cheesecloth. Cool to room temperature and refrigerate until cold.

Combine tarragon dill sauce with grated cucumber and mix well. Spoon 1/4 cup of sauce over each serving of salmon.

SERVINGS: 8. CALORIES PER SERVING: 160

TURKEY MOLE

1 large onion, finely chopped
2 cloves garlic, finely chopped
1 large fresh, ripe tomato or 3 small ones, peeled,
    seeded, and chopped
1/4 cup raisins, finely chopped
1/2 cup chopped fresh coriander (cilantro)
1/3 cup chili powder
1/3 cup carob powder
1 teaspoon salt
1 teaspoon fructose
1 teaspoon ground cinnamon
1/2 teaspoon ground cumin
1/4 teaspoon ground cloves
1/4 teaspoon anise seeds
1/4 cup unhomogenized, smooth peanut butter
3 cups Chicken Stock (see page 69)
2 pounds sliced, cooked turkey breast

Cook onion, covered, in large saucepan over low heat till soft, stirring frequently to prevent scorching. Add all other ingredients except chicken stock and turkey. Mix well and cook, uncovered, over medium heat, stirring frequently, for about 10 minutes.

Bring chicken stock to a boil in second saucepan and add it to the mole sauce. Cook, uncovered, over very low heat, stirring occasionally, for 45 minutes.

To serve, heat sliced turkey and pour 1/3 cup of sauce

over top of each serving; or chop turkey and add it to the
sauce and serve like a stew.

SERVINGS: 12. CALORIES PER SERVING: 185

FAKE FRUITCAKE

1 envelope unflavored gelatin
2 tablespoons cool water
1/4 cup boiling water
1 can (8 ounces) juice-packed crushed pineapple,
   undrained
1/4 cup instant nonfat dry milk
1 cup unsweetened applesauce
1/3 cup raisins, finely chopped
1 teaspoon carob powder
1 teaspoon ground cinnamon
1/4 teaspoon ground allspice
2 teaspoons vanilla extract
1/3 cup chopped pecans, toasted

Soften gelatin in cool water. Add boiling water and stir till
gelatin is completely dissolved.

Drain pineapple and combine juice with nonfat dry milk
in a bowl; stir mix till milk is completely dissolved. Add
pineapple and all other ingredients except pecans and mix
thoroughly. Pour mixture into lightly oiled 9-inch pie pan
and refrigerate till firm.

To serve, cut into 8 pie-shaped wedges and sprinkle top
of each serving with 2 teaspoons toasted pecans.

SERVINGS: 8. CALORIES PER SERVING: 50

GRECIAN MELON BALLS

1/4 cup frozen unsweetened apple juice concentrate, thawed
1/2 teaspoon ground anise seeds
4 cups assorted melon balls (cantaloupe, honeydew, and
    watermelon)

Combine all ingredients and mix well. Refrigerate till cold
before serving.
    SERVINGS: 8. CALORIES PER 1/2-CUP SERVING: 55

PEANUT BUTTER DELIGHT

1 cup part-skim ricotta cheese
1/4 cup unhomogenized, smooth peanut butter
2 tablespoons skim milk
2 1/4 tablespoons vanilla extract
1/2 teaspoon ground cinnamon
4 1/2 teaspoons fructose

Combine all ingredients in food processor with metal blade
and blend till satin-smooth. To serve, place a 1-ounce scoop
(2 tablespoons) in each dish.
    SERVINGS: 10. CALORIES PER SERVING: 50

PIÑA COLADA COMPOTE

1 envelope unflavored gelatin
2 tablespoons cool water
1/4 cup boiling water
1 1/2 cups skim milk
1/4 cup buttermilk
1 teaspoon ground cinnamon

1 teaspoon coconut extract
1 teaspoon vanilla extract
4 cups diced fresh pineapple or juice-packed canned
   pineapple chunks, drained

Soften gelatin in cool water. Add boiling water and stir till
gelatin is completely dissolved.

Combine gelatin mixture and all other ingredients except
pineapple in blender and blend till smooth. Refrigerate mixture in a covered container till chilled. Return to blender and
blend till it again attains a liquid consistency. Pour into a
bowl and fold in diced pineapple. Divide into 8 serving
dishes.

SERVINGS: 8. CALORIES PER 1/2-CUP SERVING: 60

FRUIT SHAKES

1/2 cup fresh fruit (see note below)
1/2 cup skim milk
1 tablespoon Protesoy powder (see note below)
1/2 cup crushed ice

Combine all ingredients in blender and blend till frothy.
Serve immediately.

SERVINGS: 1. CALORIES PER SERVING: 115

Note: If the fruit is not quite sweet enough, add 1 teaspoon fructose (and 15 calories).

Protesoy, a soy-based protein powder, is available in most
health food stores.

Canyon Ranch is fast emerging as "the serious spa" with
a variety of innovative programs for more specialized needs:

  • EXECUTIVE RENEWAL. A highly personalized week
    for business men and women, which teaches them how

to maintain good health while working and living intensely. Limited to twelve participants, this powerful experience yields high returns.

- THE ARTHRITIS PACKAGE. A week-long individual experience to help people with arthritis learn to decrease pain and increase flexibility, strength, and stamina—through exercise, massage, improved nutrition, and stress management.
- LIFESTYLE MODIFICATION SERIES. Tailored to each individual's personal goals, this series of private consultations with staff professionals is designed to help people permanently eliminate unwanted behaviors related to smoking, weight, exercise, and stress. This program gets you started and keeps you motivated to change for life.

Already the spa with a larger male clientele than any other, Canyon Ranch continues to expand its men's programs. The Men's Action Package has been added to the regular spa package and includes a more active program for the sports enthusiast. The popular seven- and ten-night packages provide a healthy combination of personal consultations, massages, herbal wraps, facials, beauty service of your choice—and include lodging, three gourmet meals per day, and use of all facilities. Special holiday, family, and group discounts are available.

The Wooden Door

Secluded in fifty-four wooded acres on Wisconsin's beautiful Lake Geneva, the Wooden Door is the Midwest's affordable alternative to the posh spas found elsewhere.

Although its name is a good-natured parody of the exclusive Golden Door in California, the agenda at the Wooden Door is no joke—it's a serious program designed to give women a running start on a healthy life through a wholesome diet and a variety of exercise programs.

The decor is rustic, in keeping with the natural surroundings. Guests sleep in cabins that can accommodate six but are generally used for only three or four women at a time. There are no telephones or television sets in the cabins; there are, however, bathrooms with hot and cold running water. The facilities are simple, but not primitive.

The philosophy behind all this austerity is simple—it keeps costs down and encourages guests to get out of their rooms and into a wide range of daily activities, although none of the Wooden Door's activities are required. A guest whose idea of exercise is sunning on the pier or reading by the pool is free to do so.

Guests arrive at the Wooden Door on Sunday afternoon between 3:00 and 5:00 P.M. They are weighed and measured in private. It's the last time a guest will see a scale all week, thus eliminating any chance of discouragement or depression if no weight loss is evident the first few days (a common occurrence).

Dinner, consisting of about 350 calories, is followed by an outline of the exercise programs and beauty clinics available, and some general advice about dieting. The Wooden Door's owners and operators, Jill Adzia, Shirley McAlear, and Naomi Stark, stress the importance of drinking water (twelve 8-ounce glasses per day) to flush out wastes and provide the proper hydration for exercise.

A day at the Wooden Door starts with a beginner's yoga session at sunrise and a walk or jog along a section of the spa's twenty-six miles of woodland trails. After breakfast, more yoga (intermediate) is available, as are exercise classes led by McAlear, a physical fitness teacher for over ten years, and Stark, an experienced runner and aerobic dance instructor.

Some classes are fast paced, others are relaxed; all are accompanied by music and held either in the air-conditioned gymnasium or the wooden gazebo jutting out into the lake. The Wooden Door also offers modern ballet classes for non-ballet dancers. These are taught by Adzia, formerly a dance instructor.

Stark, a graduate of the Dumas Père Cooking School, has planned the Wooden Door's menus with an emphasis on sound nutrition, easy preparation, and eye-appeal.

Breakfast can be as simple as whole-grain cereal, skim milk, and grapefruit, melon, or raisins. A tasty muffin or mushroom omelet is only a shade more complicated.

THE RIGHT BLUEBERRY MUFFINS

2 tablespoons vegetable oil
1 to 1 1/2 tablespoons honey
1 egg, beaten
1 1/2 cups whole-wheat flour
3/4 cup unbleached all-purpose flour
2 teaspoons baking powder
1/2 cup skim milk
1/4 cup fresh blueberries
1/4 teaspoon freshly grated nutmeg
1/2 teaspoon grated lemon zest

Preheat oven to 400 degrees.

Mix oil and honey in bowl. Add egg. Stir in remaining ingredients and spoon into muffin cups lined with paper liners, filling each no more than two-thirds full. Bake for 25 minutes, or till tops spring back when touched.

MAKES 9 MUFFINS. CALORIES PER MUFFIN: 150

MUSHROOM OMELET

1 egg plus 1 egg white
1 teaspoon minced onion
1 tablespoon chopped fresh mushrooms
1/4 cup low-fat cottage cheese
1 teaspoon vegetable oil

Separate egg; beat whites till frothy and yolk till thick and lemon-colored. Gently fold yolk into whites. Add onion, mushrooms, and cottage cheese. Heat oil in skillet till it sizzles. Pour in mixture, spreading it evenly over the skillet. Cook till mixture is puffed and set. Make a shallow cut in the center with spatula. Tilt pan, and fold upper half of omelet over lower half. Serve immediately.

SERVINGS: 1. CALORIES PER SERVING: 150

Herb tea is served at meals at the Wooden Door. Coffee, though available, is discouraged by the staff, as caffeine is thought to be an appetite stimulant. When more than sparkling cold water (with fresh lemons) is desired, guests may indulge in warm or cold punch, or try Mock Sangria.

WARM CITRUS PUNCH

12 whole cloves
2 cinnamon sticks (2 inches each)
2 whole nutmegs
4 cups unsweetened apple cider
3 cups unsweetened orange juice
3 cups unsweetened grapefruit juice
Juice of 1 lemon
Garnish: 1 slice each grapefruit, orange, and lemon
Sparkling water (optional)

Tie spices in a cheesecloth bag or place in a tea ball. Add to cider in a large saucepan and simmer for 10 to 15 minutes. Remove and discard spices. Add citrus juices to saucepan and reheat till just warm. Garnish with cut fruit to serve.

SERVINGS: 20. CALORIES PER 1/2-CUP SERVING: 50

Note: Punch can also be served cold, with sparkling water, if desired.

MOCK SANGRIA

1 quart unsweetened grape juice
Juice of 2 oranges
Juice of 1 lemon

1 quart sparkling water (not club soda)
1/2 orange, thinly sliced
1/2 lemon, thinly sliced
1 lime, thinly sliced

Mix juices and sparkling water; add fruit and chill thoroughly.

SERVINGS: 10. CALORIES PER 1-CUP SERVING: 85

Dinner is the midday meal at the Wooden Door. Dinner and supper menus are interchangeable, but the staff suggests that the larger meal be eaten earlier in the day. As hot soups with acid ingredients such as tomatoes or cabbage tend to curb the appetite, these are served often. The Wooden Door's Minestrone is a good, and filling, example:

MINESTRONE

1 cup dried white beans
4 cups water
2 tablespoons vegetable oil
2 cups finely chopped onion
1 tablespoon minced garlic
1 to 1 1/2 cups finely shredded, thoroughly cleaned leeks
3 cups finely shredded cabbage
2 cups finely chopped carrots
2 zucchini (about 8 ounces), quartered and sliced
    lengthwise
2 fresh, ripe tomatoes (about 12 ounces), peeled, seeded,
    and cut into 1-inch cubes
1/2 cup finely chopped fresh parsley
1/4 cup finely chopped fresh basil or 1 tablespoon dried
1 teaspoon finely chopped fresh rosemary or 1/2
    teaspoon dried
4 cups bouillon
3/4 cup small macaroni, preferably ditalini

Unless no soaking is specified on the package, put beans in a bowl and add water till about 2 inches above top of beans. Let soak overnight.

Drain beans; put them in a soup kettle and add 4 cups water. Bring to a boil, cover, and simmer for 50 minutes to 1 hour, or till beans are tender. Drain, saving 2 cups of liquid.

Heat oil in a large saucepan; add onion. Sauté, stirring, till onion is wilted; add garlic and stir. Add leeks, cabbage, carrots, zucchini, and tomatoes. Cook, stirring occasionally, for about 10 minutes. Add parsley, basil, rosemary, reserved bean liquid, and bouillon. Purée half the beans in food processor, food mill, or blender; add to soup, along with remaining beans. Bring to a boil and simmer for 25 minutes.

Add macaroni and cook 15 minutes longer, or till macaroni is tender. Serve immediately.

SERVINGS: 10. CALORIES PER SERVING: 150

BROWN RICE SALAD

1/3 cup diced carrots
1/4 cup diced celery
1/4 cup diced green bell pepper
3/4 cup sliced (1/4 inch) green beans, blanched or
    raw
1/2 cup frozen green peas
1/4 cup chopped red onion
3 tablespoons minced fresh parsley
2 1/4 cups cooked brown rice, without salt (cooked with
    1/2 cup water and 1/2 cup orange juice)
1/4 cup grated low-fat cheese, such as mozzarella
3 tablespoons white wine vinegar
1/4 cup vegetable oil (optional)
Salt (optional)
Freshly ground black pepper
1/8 teaspoon dried thyme

1/8 teaspoon dried basil
1/8 teaspoon dried oregano
Large green lettuce leaves

Combine first 8 ingredients in a large bowl and mix well.
Blend cheese, vinegar, seasonings, and oil (if desired) in a
blender or large jar. Pour over rice mixture and toss till
thoroughly combined. Refrigerate for several hours. Serve
mounded on a few large lettuce leaves.

SERVINGS: 4. CALORIES PER SERVING: 95

ORANGE AND LETTUCE SALAD

2 large heads dark green lettuce
3 large oranges
1 small red onion
3/4 cup finely chopped fresh parsley
1 cup Orange Vinaigrette (recipe follows)
1/2 teaspoon celery seeds

Have all ingredients chilled and place in a chilled salad bowl
as each is prepared. Tear lettuce into bite-size pieces. Carefully section oranges, removing membranes; halve each orange section, removing any seeds. Slice onion into paper-thin
rings. Add parsley. Toss with the vinaigrette, then sprinkle
with celery seeds and toss again.

SERVINGS: 6. CALORIES PER SERVING: 70

ORANGE VINAIGRETTE

1 cup mild vinegar
2 cloves garlic, minced or mashed
2 teaspoons frozen orange juice concentrate, thawed
1 teaspoon dry mustard
1/2 teaspoon freshly ground white pepper

Place all ingredients in blender or food processor and blend for 10 seconds. Chill before serving.

MAKES ABOUT 1 CUP. CALORIES PER TABLESPOON: 5

PEA AND PIMIENTO SALAD

1 package (10 ounces) frozen peas, thawed
3 ounces canned pimiento, drained and chopped
4 ounces canned water chestnuts, drained and chopped
1/2 cup finely chopped scallions
1/2 cup plain low-fat yogurt, thoroughly drained (the
    thicker the better)
1/4 teaspoon freshly ground black pepper
Pinch dried chervil

Combine all ingredients and refrigerate 1 to 2 days before serving on red leaf lettuce.

SERVINGS: 6. CALORIES PER SERVING: 115

Note: Other nice additions to this salad include celery, Jerusalem artichokes, carrots, and green bell pepper. Vary color and texture, but be careful not to use vegetables that will secrete too much water.

Entrées for dinner and supper frequently feature vegetarian dishes—the Wooden Door's menus contain much less protein, especially high-cholesterol animal protein, than the usual American meals. No red meat is served. Fish, poultry, and vegetable-based entrées are also lower in calories.

PASTA WITH FRESH GREEN SAUCE

2 cups small-curd, low-fat cottage cheese
1 bunch watercress, washed, stemmed, and chopped
2 cucumbers, peeled, seeded, and chopped

3 scallions, finely chopped
Freshly ground black pepper, dried oregano, and dried
    basil to taste
1 pound whole-wheat, spinach, or Jerusalem artichoke
    pasta

Combine cheese, vegetables, and seasonings and mix well.
Let stand at room temperature to blend flavors.

Meanwhile, cook pasta in large saucepan of boiling water
according to package directions. Drain, then rinse under
cold running water to remove excess starch. Toss with
cheese/vegetable mixture and serve immediately.

SERVINGS: 6. CALORIES PER SERVING: 180

Note: May also be served cold.

HEARTY VEGETABLE CHILI

1 onion, chopped
1 clove garlic, minced
1 green bell pepper, seeded and chopped
1 cup corn kernels (preferably fresh or fresh frozen)
Up to 2 cups liquid (you can use salt-free bouillon, liquid
    from canned tomatoes or steamed vegetables, tomato
    juice, or sugar-free canned tomato sauce)
1 cup seeded and chopped tomatoes
1 can (6 ounces) sugar-free tomato paste
4 cups cooked kidney or pinto beans
1 1/2 tablespoons chili powder
1/4 teaspoon ground cumin
1 teaspoon dried oregano

Sauté onion and garlic without fat in nonstick skillet until
onion is translucent. Add green pepper and sauté another 2
to 3 minutes. Add corn, half of liquid (reserve remainder to
add later, if desired), tomatoes, and tomato paste.

Mash 2 cups of beans and add to pot along with remaining whole beans and seasonings. Cover and simmer 30 minutes. Add more of the liquid, if necessary. If chili is too watery, remove lid and cook until thickened. Serve accompanied by one or more of the following:

Chopped lettuce
Chopped scallions
Chopped tomatoes
Chopped fresh green chilies
Grated low-fat cheese

SERVINGS: 6. CALORIES PER 1/2-CUP SERVING: 150
Note: Can also be stuffed into corn tortillas and eaten out of hand.

PITA PIZZA

1 white-flour or whole-wheat pita bread, cut into
    quarters
1/4 cup tomato paste (preferably low sodium)
1/4 cup tomato sauce (preferably low sodium)
1/2 teaspoon dried basil
1/2 teaspoon dried oregano
1/8 teaspoon garlic powder
1/8 teaspoon onion powder
4 tablespoons farmers cheese or dry-curd cottage cheese
Optional garnish: Green bell pepper, onion, or
    mushrooms

Preheat oven to 350 degrees.
    Place wedges of pita, browned side down, on a baking sheet. Mix tomato paste and sauce; spread over pita. Blend seasonings with cheese. Put about 1 tablespoon of cheese/spice mixture over sauce on each pita quarter. Bake

about 10 to 15 minutes, or till cheese is slightly melted and bottom is crisp. Optional vegetables can be added before or after baking.

SERVINGS: 4. CALORIES PER SERVING: 150

CRUSTLESS SPINACH QUICHE

1 package (10 ounces) frozen chopped spinach
2 teaspoons chopped onion
1 clove garlic, minced
1 cup shredded low-fat cheese
2 tablespoons unbleached all-purpose flour
1/2 teaspoon either freshly grated nutmeg, dried sage,
    dried tarragon, or dried basil
2 medium-size eggs, lightly beaten, or egg substitute, or
    whole egg plus 1 egg white
1 cup skim milk
Paprika

Preheat oven to 350 degrees.

Cook spinach in saucepan according to package directions, omitting salt. Drain well; keep liquid for use as soup stock. Sauté onion and garlic without fat in nonstick skillet until onion is translucent. Mix cheese, flour, and herbs in small bowl.

Combine eggs or egg substitute and milk in a large bowl; add spinach, sautéed onion and garlic, and cheese mixture. Mix well, then pour into a nonstick 9-inch pie or quiche pan or 8-inch square pan. Dust with paprika. Bake about 40 minutes, or till center is firm to touch.

SERVINGS: 6. CALORIES PER SERVING: 120

CHICKEN BREASTS WITH MUSHROOM SAUCE

2 chicken breasts (6 to 8 ounces each), halved, skinned, and
      boned (dressed weight, about 4 ounces each)
1/2 cup canned evaporated skim milk
1 cup fine whole-wheat bread crumbs
2 cups sliced fresh mushrooms
2 tablespoons diced scallions
1/2 cup dry white wine
1 teaspoon lemon juice
1/8 teaspoon dried thyme
1/8 teaspoon dried marjoram

Preheat oven to 350 degrees.
      Pound chicken breasts with a meat mallet. Dip each in
milk, then bread crumbs, covering well. Roll up and arrange,
seam down, in nonstick baking pan. Cover and bake for 25
minutes.
      Meanwhile, simmer mushrooms and scallions, uncov-
ered, in wine and lemon juice in a skillet until tender; stir in
seasonings. Uncover baking pan and spoon sautéed vegetables over each rolled-up chicken breast. Bake, uncovered, 10
minutes longer, or till chicken is tender and brown.
      SERVINGS: 4. CALORIES PER SERVING: 210

ARTICHOKES AND SCALLOPS WITH DILL SAUCE

1 clove garlic, peeled and halved
1 thick lemon slice
Few black peppercorns
4 artichokes, trimmed and stems removed
2 cups bay scallops

1/2 cup chopped celery
1/2 cup chopped green bell pepper
1 1/3 cups Dill Sauce (recipe follows)
Garnish: 4 lemon slices or fresh parsley sprigs

Add garlic, lemon, and peppercorns to a saucepan filled to a depth of 1 inch with water. Bring water to a boil and add artichokes, setting upright. Cover tightly, then reduce heat to medium and cook for about 40 minutes, or till artichoke bottoms are tender when pierced with a fork. Drain artichokes upside down until cool enough to handle. Remove center leaves and chokes.

Steam scallops for 3 to 5 minutes, or till they turn an opaque white. Combine with celery, green pepper, and 2/3 cup of the dill sauce. Divide mixture among artichokes. Garnish each with a lemon slice or parsley sprig and serve, using remaining dill sauce as a dip for artichoke leaves.

SERVINGS: 4. CALORIES PER SERVING: 180

DILL SAUCE

2 cups plain low-fat yogurt, drained
4 teaspoons frozen unsweetened apple juice concentrate, thawed
4 teaspoons dried dillweed
Freshly ground black pepper
Red wine vinegar (only enough to balance sweetness)

Combine all ingredients thoroughly with a whisk.

MAKES 2 TO 2 1/2 CUPS. CALORIES PER TABLESPOON: 12

And, yes, there are desserts and snacks—not only fresh fruits and vegetables, but also goodies like Easy Frozen Yogurt, Mocha Ice, Poached Pears with Fruit Sauce, or Cheese Tart.

EASY FROZEN YOGURT

1 large banana, peeled and then frozen
1/2 cup plain low-fat yogurt
1/4 cup unsweetened pineapple juice
1/2 cup fresh berries or peeled, sliced peaches
Garnish: Fresh berries or peeled, sliced peaches

Slice banana and place in blender or food processor; add yogurt and pineapple juice, blending till smooth and thick. Add berries and blend again. Serve immediately or freeze till firm. Thaw 15 minutes before serving, garnished with berries or peaches.

SERVINGS: 4. CALORIES PER SERVING: 75

MOCHA ICE

3 heaping teaspoons carob powder
2 heaping teaspoons Postum, Pero, or Caffix (coffee substitutes; see note below)
3 heaping teaspoons instant nonfat dry milk
1/4 cup water
Ice cubes

Add dry ingredients to water in blender and mix briefly. Add a few ice cubes. With blender set on high, turn on and off till most of the ice is chopped. Add more cubes, repeat till machine grinds cubes completely. When mixture is as thick as you wish, spoon out and serve immediately, or allow to harden in freezer.

SERVINGS: 4. CALORIES PER SERVING: 50

Note: If you wish to use decaffeinated coffee, use Brim, Sanka, or Taster's Choice.

POACHED PEARS WITH FRUIT SAUCE

2 pears, halved and cored
1/2 cup unsweetened apple juice
1/2 cup water
1 cinnamon stick
6 whole cloves
1 whole nutmeg
2 dates, pitted and thinly sliced
4 teaspoons plain low-fat yogurt
Ground cinnamon or freshly grated nutmeg (optional)
Garnish: 4 lemon slices

Trim bottom of pears so that they will sit flat. Place in a small saucepan; add juice, water, and spices. Cover and bring to a boil, then reduce heat and simmer for 5 to 10 minutes, or till pears are tender. Remove pears from juice. After straining out cinnamon stick, cloves, and nutmeg, add dates. Spoon date mixture into pear cavity and top with a dollop of yogurt. Sprinkle with cinnamon or nutmeg, if desired. Garnish with lemon slices.

SERVINGS: 4. CALORIES PER SERVING: 75

CHEESE TART

1 cup Grape-Nuts cereal
Frozen unsweetened apple juice concentrate, thawed, to
    thin
1 can (16 ounces) unsweetened crushed pineapple,
    undrained
1 envelope unflavored gelatin
1 2/3 cups part-skim ricotta cheese or low-fat cottage
    cheese
1/2 teaspoon vanilla extract
Ground cinnamon (optional)
1 bag (16 ounces) dry-pack frozen blueberries
2 tablespoons arrowroot or cornstarch
1/2 cup cold water
1/2 teaspoon almond extract (optional)

Crush cereal in blender or food processor till crumblike in
consistency. Mix in only enough apple juice concentrate so
mixture can be pressed into a nonstick 12-inch pie or tart pan.
Chill while you prepare filling.

Pour 1/2 cup pineapple juice from canned pineapple into
a saucepan. Sprinkle gelatin on top to soften, heating gently
to dissolve. Combine pineapple, extra juice (if any), cheese,
and vanilla (plus cinnamon, if desired) in blender or food
processor. Process till very creamy. Add gelatin mixture and
mix till smooth. Pour into chilled shell. Process three fourths
of the berries and about 2 tablespoons of apple juice concentrate till you have a thick purée; reserve remaining berries
for decoration. Mix arrowroot with cold water until dissolved; add to berry purée in saucepan. Cook, uncovered,
over low heat till gel-like in consistency. Remove from heat
and stir in optional almond extract; let cool. Spread over
cheese filling. Refrigerate till filling and topping are set, at
least 3 hours.

Before serving, decorate outer edge with remaining berries.

SERVINGS: 12. CALORIES PER SERVING: 120

For those who simply cannot adhere to the 900-calorie-a-day diet, the Wooden Door stocks a supplementary table set with muffins, cheese, peanut butter, and skim milk.

Between meals and classes, guests can enjoy water sports on the lake—swimming, boating, skiing, and fishing—or tennis, volleyball, and shuffleboard on land. Beauty and fashion clinics and career development and assertiveness seminars are conducted during the day, and special programs such as square dances and boat rides are planned for evening entertainment.

The Wooden Door is sixty-five miles from Chicago at Covenant Harbor, one half mile west of Lake Geneva, Wisconsin, on Wisconsin Highway 50. Who comes to the Wooden Door? Women from eighteen to seventy; some slim, some obese; some fit, some not. But all leave this special, unpretentious retreat with a new lease on life.

National Institute
of Fitness

T hree hundred miles south of Salt Lake City and 120 miles
north of Las Vegas there is a geological paradise known
as Color Country—blue skies reflected in the deeper blues of
Lake Powell, shades of green ranging from the silvery aspens
to the darkest pines of Zion National Park, and the red and
gold cliffs of Bryce Canyon and Grand Canyon. Here, at the
mouth of Snow Canyon, Marcus B. Sorenson, Ed.D., has
founded and, with his wife, Vicki, directs the National Institute of Fitness. St. George, where the Institute is located,
commonly referred to as Utah's Dixie or "The Other Palm
Springs," is an ideal year-round vacation spot with its moderate climate and access to the warm desert in winter and the
cool Pine Valley Mountain forests in summer.

The National Institute of Fitness (NIF) is dedicated to
eliminating obesity, the nation's number one health prob-
lem. Stress-related conditions such as diabetes, hypo-
glycemia, hypertension, and ulcers often improve substan-

tially with a stay in this beautiful, restful environment, aided by the Institute's threefold agenda of nutrition, education, and exercise.

Sorenson, also known as Dr. Fit, has developed a reducing program based on Slim Nutrition and lots of "Vitamin X" (exercise). Walking is one of the best ways to take Vitamin X, but guests at the Institute also participate in aerobics, cycling, swimnastics, and other sports according to each one's ability and fitness level. Because of Vitamin X, pounds lost at the Institute are often exceeded by inches lost. Overweight guests from fourteen to eighty-four experience higher self-esteem as a result of their new trim appearance and the knowledge that they can control their weight.

Programs begin on Mondays, when each guest undergoes a Personal Fitness Evaluation that includes a cardiovascular fitness evaluation; weight, strength, and fitness tests; a blood pressure test; and determination of body fat composition. Mornings start with a walk or hike before breakfast, which usually consists of whole-grain cereal served with a small portion of fruit (1/3 banana, 1/2 apple or grapefruit, 1/4 cup strawberries), and 6 ounces of skim milk. Two medium-size pancakes, waffles, or muffins may be substituted for the cereal.

PANCAKES AND WAFFLE MIX

2 cups whole-wheat flour
1/2 cup instant nonfat dry milk
1/2 cup whey (optional; see note below)
1/2 cup powdered egg white
6 packets Equal
1 tablespoon baking powder

Mix all ingredients and store in an airtight container. To prepare, add water till desired consistency is achieved. Cook on a hot griddle sprayed lightly with low-calorie vegetable coating. For waffles, use 1/2 cup per waffle.

MAKES 10 3-INCH PANCAKES. CALORIES PER 2-PANCAKE SERVING: 204

Variation: One-half cup of any of the following may be added to the batter: cooked or dry oatmeal, blueberries, mashed bananas, or chopped apple; or 1 teaspoon ground cinnamon.

Note: Available in health food stores.

PINEAPPLE BRAN MUFFINS

1 cup Pancake or Waffle Mix (see preceding recipe)
1 cup All Bran
1/2 cup canned, juice-packed, crushed pineapple, drained

Preheat oven to 350 degrees.

Combine pancake mix and All Bran.

Add enough water to just moisten mixture. Do not over-mix. Spray 6 muffin cups with low-calorie vegetable coating. Place 1 tablespoon crushed pineapple in bottom of each cup and cover with the muffin batter. Bake for 20 to 30 minutes.

MAKES 12 MUFFINS. CALORIES PER MUFFIN: 70

Guests are given a bag lunch to carry on the daily midmorning walk. This bag meal is usually a small piece of fruit, a plastic sandwich bag filled with raw or steamed vegetables, and one ounce of chicken, turkey, or waterpack tuna. Some guests prefer to use part of their lunch as a midmorning or afternoon snack. There is no food served between meals at the Institute.

Sorenson suggests that eating three meals a day, then forgetting about food, is one of the fundamentals of fat control. He urges guests to stop counting food calories and instead be concerned about counting exercise calories, stressing that "preoccupation with exercise is the surest and fastest psychological means to success." Exercise reduces hunger pangs by raising the blood sugar level and drawing blood to muscles and away from digestive areas. It increases the rate at which food is metabolized and also burns calories directly. Dr. Fit emphasizes that daily exercise is more important than any other habit.

Group exercise classes and sports are scheduled for afternoon activity. No guest is required to participate, although those who do lose pounds and inches faster. The facilities at the NIF include modern cardiovascular and weight-training equipment and the largest indoor pool in southern Utah.

Dinner, like breakfast, is ample; meals here are low in calories but high in volume. Guests who are hungry are urged to ask for something more to eat. There is no red meat served; however, the vegetarian, poultry, and seafood recipes created by Chef Howard Gifford are attractive and appetizing and give great variety to the Institute's menus.

CHEESE STUFFED BAKED POTATO

4 medium-size baking potatoes
1 scallion, diced
1 small onion, minced
1/2 teaspoon freshly ground white pepper
1 teaspoon onion powder
1/4 teaspoon dry mustard
1 cup skim milk
8 ounces Monterey Jack cheese, shredded
Garnish: 8 cherry tomatoes

Preheat oven to 425 degrees.

Bake potatoes for 1 1/4 hours. Remove from oven (leaving oven on at 425 degrees) and cut in halves horizontally. Scoop out potato flesh and place in medium-size mixing

bowl; reserve potato shells. Add scallion, onion, and spices
and mix on medium speed. Heat milk, and add slowly to
mixture, then whip on high speed for 30 seconds. Spoon
mashed potato mixture into reserved potato shells. Place
stuffed potatoes in a 9-inch square baking dish and sprinkle
each potato sparingly with cheese. Brown in oven. Garnish
each potato with a cherry tomato and serve.

SERVINGS: 8. CALORIES PER SERVING: 152

STUFFED CABBAGE ROLL

1 firm head green cabbage
1 medium-size onion, minced
1 green bell pepper, seeded and minced
1 cup minced fresh mushrooms
1 pound ground uncooked turkey
1 cup cooked and cooled brown rice
1 cup cold, defatted turkey broth
1 tablespoon vegetable salt
1 tablespoon onion powder
1 tablespoon garlic powder
1 teaspoon curry powder
1/2 teaspoon dry mustard
1/4 teaspoon freshly ground white pepper
1 can (6 ounces) salt-free tomato paste
2 cups Tangy Tomato Sauce (recipe follows)

Parboil cabbage till soft. Invert onto dry towel to drain and
let cool.

Preheat oven to 350 degrees.

Peel 8 large leaves from cabbage head and lay out flat on
clean surface. Mix remaining ingredients together and divide
into 8 even portions. Place each in the center of a leaf and
roll from steam end, folding in sides after first roll. Spray a

shallow baking pan with a low-calorie vegetable coating.
Arrange cabbage rolls in pan and bake for 40 minutes.

Serve immediately, pouring 1/4 cup Tangy Tomato
Sauce over each roll.

SERVINGS: 8. CALORIES PER SERVING: 222

TANGY TOMATO SAUCE

2 cans (15 ounces each) salt-free tomato sauce
1 tablespoon dried basil
1 bay leaf
1 teaspoon garlic powder
1 cup skim milk
Dash red wine vinegar

Bring tomato sauce to a slow boil in saucepan over medium
heat. Stir in seasonings, then reduce heat to a simmer. Add
milk and vinegar and simmer till heated through.

SERVINGS: 8. CALORIES PER SERVING: 42

TURKEY SPINACH SOUFFLÉ ROLL

2 pounds spinach (see note below)
2 scallions, chopped
4 egg whites
1/4 teaspoon freshly grated nutmeg
1 cup imitation sour cream
1 cup freshly grated Parmesan cheese
1 cup ground, cooked turkey
1 shallot or scallion, chopped
3 tablespoons chopped fresh parsley
Optional garnish: 2 tablespoons imitation sour cream and
        1 teaspoon chopped fresh chives

Preheat oven to 350 degrees. Spray a 15 × 10-inch jelly-roll pan with low-calorie vegetable coating, then line pan with wax paper and spray paper with coating.

Discard stems and bruised leaves from spinach; wash thoroughly in cold water. Drain well, then chop. Cook spinach and chopped scallions, covered, in large skillet till spinach is slightly wilted. Drain.

Beat egg whites in large bowl until soft peaks form. Beat in nutmeg, 1/3 cup of the imitation sour cream, and 1/2 cup of the cheese, then stir spinach mixture into bowl. Pour soufflé mixture into prepared baking pan; sprinkle with remaining 1/2 cup cheese. Bake 30 to 35 minutes, or till top springs back when lightly touched.

Invert pan immediately on a kitchen towel. Remove pan and peel wax paper from soufflé. Combine remaining 2/3 cup sour cream, the turkey, shallot, and parsley. Spread this over soufflé. Roll up jelly-roll fashion from long side, then garnish, if desired, and serve.

SERVINGS: 8. CALORIES PER SERVING: 174

Note: 2 packages (10 ounces each) frozen chopped spinach can be used instead of fresh spinach. Thaw and drain thoroughly before adding to shallot and chopped scallions.

TURKEY LASAGNE

4 cups defatted turkey stock
8 small fresh, ripe tomatoes, peeled
1 tablespoon garlic powder
1 tablespoon onion powder
1 teaspoon dried thyme
1 teaspoon dried oregano
1 teaspoon dried rosemary
1 teaspoon dried basil
1 bay leaf
Pinch freshly ground white pepper

1 pound ground turkey
2 medium-size onions, diced
1 green bell pepper, seeded and diced
1 cup diced fresh mushrooms
1 can (15 ounces) salt-free tomato paste
1 teaspoon low-fat vegetable oil
1 package (8 ounces) non-egg lasagne noodles
1 cup strained nonfat cottage cheese
1 cup shredded Monterey Jack cheese

Combine stock, tomatoes, and seasonings in a 2-quart saucepan. Cover and bring to a boil, then reduce heat and simmer
2 hours. Remove from heat.

Combine ground turkey, onions, green pepper, and
mushrooms in a skillet and sauté without fat till glazed. Drain
well, then add to tomato stock along with tomato paste and
simmer another 30 minutes. Remove from heat and let cool.
Bring 3 quarts water to a boil with vegetable oil in a 4-quart
saucepan. Add lasagne, a strip at a time, and continue boiling
10 to 12 minutes, or till tender. As lasagne cooks, separate
strips with a fork to keep noodles from sticking. Remove
from heat and drain.

Preheat oven to 300 degrees.

In a 13 × 9-inch baking dish sprayed with low-fat vegetable coating, put one layer of lasagne noodles, overlapping
each strip. Add enough sauce just to cover first layer. Sprinkle 1/4 cup of cottage cheese and 1/4 cup of Jack cheese
evenly over sauce. Repeat the above to create 4 layers. Cover
top with remaining sauce. Bake for 40 minutes. Remove and
let stand 10 to 15 minutes to allow layers to set. Cut into
3-inch squares to serve.

SERVINGS: 12. CALORIES PER SERVING: 232

STUFFED TURKEY ROLLS WITH CREAM GRAVY

Turkey Rolls:
8 slices preservative-free whole-wheat bread, diced
1 medium-size onion, diced
1 celery stalk, trimmed and diced
1 tablespoon ground or rubbed sage
1 tablespoon vegetable salt
1 tablespoon onion powder
1/2 teaspoon freshly ground white pepper
1 cup defatted turkey stock
8 turkey patty steaks

Cream Turkey Gravy:
4 cups defatted turkey stock
1/2 cup arrowroot or cornstarch
3 cups water
2 tablespoons vegetable salt
1 tablespoon onion powder
Pinch freshly ground white pepper
4 ounces white-meat turkey (optional but recommended),
    puréed
1 cup hot skim milk
Garnish: Chopped fresh parsley

Preheat oven to 375 degrees.

Combine bread, onion, celery, and seasonings in medium-size bowl; add stock and mix well. Place stuffing mixture in shallow nonstick baking dish (or spray with low-fat vegetable coating). Bake for 35 minutes, or till golden brown. Remove from oven (reduce oven heat to 350 degrees) and let cool.

Lay turkey patties out flat on plastic wrap; cover with another sheet of plastic wrap. Using meat mallet, pound patties till double original size. Remove plastic wrap and cut patties in half. Divide stuffing into 16 portions. Place one portion in center of each patty; roll patty up. Set rolls aside while you make gravy.

Bring 4 cups stock to a boil in a large saucepan. Stir water into arrowroot or cornstarch in bowl and mix well. Add mixture to stock slowly, stirring constantly, then reduce heat to low. Add seasonings and puréed turkey to stock, then slowly stir in hot milk. Let simmer, uncovered, for 30 minutes.

Meanwhile, spray a 13 × 9-inch baking pan with low-fat vegetable coating. Arrange turkey rolls in pan and bake for 20 minutes.

To serve, ladle 1/4 cup gravy over each roll. Sprinkle with parsley and serve immediately.

SERVINGS: 8. CALORIES PER SERVING: 195

Note: Leftover gravy can be frozen for another use; there are 108 calories per 1/4 cup.

Desserts are prepared using the same kinds of wholesome ingredients found in the other recipes—whole grains, fruits, and vegetables.

APPLE-CARROT PUDDING

8 medium-size green apples, peeled, cored, and grated
2 cups finely grated carrots
1/2 cup brown sugar substitute (found in most health food stores) mixed with 1 teaspoon ground cinnamon
1/4 cup grated orange zest
1/4 cup grated lemon zest
12 slices preservative-free whole-wheat bread, dried out in oven and crushed into crumbs
2 tablespoons cholesterol-free egg product

Preheat oven to 350 degrees.

Combine all ingredients in large bowl, then turn into 13 × 9-inch baking pan sprayed with low-fat vegetable coating. Place pan into a 15 × 11-inch baking pan; fill larger pan with water to come halfway up sides. Bake pudding for 45 minutes.

Serve warm, with Yogurt Fruit Topping (recipe follows).

SERVINGS: 8. CALORIES PER SERVING: 103

YOGURT FRUIT TOPPING

2 cups plain low-fat yogurt
1/4 cup Grape-Nuts cereal
1 1/2 cups unsweetened pineapple juice
Juice of 2 1/2 lemons
1 teaspoon vanilla extract
1/2 teaspoon coconut extract
Low-calorie sweetener to taste

Fold all ingredients gently together. Serve with Apple-Carrot Pudding (see preceding recipe) or over a variety of fruits.

MAKES ABOUT 4 CUPS. CALORIES PER TABLESPOON: 47

PINEAPPLE BANANA CHEESE "PIE"

1/2 cup Grape-Nuts cereal
1 cup canned juice-packed crushed pineapple, drained
3 ripe bananas, sliced
1 1/2 cups unsweetened pineapple juice
1 cup low-fat cottage cheese
3 packets low-calorie sweetener
1 envelope unflavored gelatin
Milk

Sprinkle Grape-Nuts over bottom of a 9-inch square pan. Layer with pineapple and then bananas.

Blend together pineapple juice, cottage cheese, and sweetener. Soften gelatin with just enough milk to dissolve it. Blend into cheese mixture and pour over top of fruit. Chill for 5 or 6 hours.

SERVINGS: 14. CALORIES PER SERVING: 85

Variation: Instead of pineapple, use 2 cups waterpack cherries, sweetened with 15 packets of low-calorie sweetener and thickened with 1/2 teaspoon gelatin. Add 1 teaspoon almond extract.

ALMOST HEAVEN TOPPING

1/2 cup milk
Pinch cream of tartar
Few drops vanilla extract, or to taste
10 to 15 packets low-calorie sweetener

Combine all ingredients and chill in the freezer till ice crystals form; beat at high speed until light and fluffy. For added stiffness add 1/4 teaspoon (3 calories) unflavored gelatin. Serve as a dessert, in sherbet dishes, or as a topping.

SERVINGS: 15. CALORIES PER SERVING: 5

CAROB TOPPING

1/2 cup carob powder
1 teaspoon cornstarch
1/2 teaspoon unflavored gelatin
1/2 cup water
6 to 8 packets low-calorie sweetener

Combine all ingredients in a small saucepan and cook over medium heat till slightly thickened. Allow to cool, then drizzle a small amount over individual servings of ice cream.

MAKES ABOUT 2/3 CUP. CALORIES PER TABLESPOON: 12

GELATIN DESSERT

2 cups unsweetened fruit juice (any flavor)
1 tablespoon unflavored gelatin

Sprinkle gelatin with fruit juice in small saucepan; heat till gelatin is dissolved. Chill till set.

SERVINGS: 8. CALORIES PER SERVING: 85

Variations: Add fruit to the gelatin and layer with Almost Heaven Topping (see page 113) in parfait glasses; or layer different flavors (chill each flavor till set before pouring another layer over).

APPLES LORRAINE

6 apples, peeled, cored, and chopped
2 teaspoons ground cinnamon
2 tablespoons cornstarch
2 tablespoons frozen unsweetened apple juice concentrate, thawed
1/2 cup Grape-Nuts cereal
Almost Heaven Topping (optional; see page 113)

Preheat oven to 325 degrees.

Toss chopped apples with cinnamon and cornstarch. Stir in apple juice concentrate. Place in a casserole dish sprayed with low-fat vegetable coating. Sprinkle Grape-Nuts over apple mixture and bake 20 to 25 minutes. Serve topped with Almost Heaven Topping, if desired.

SERVINGS: 8. CALORIES PER SERVING: 80 (WITH TOPPING)

Fruit juices are used sparingly in recipes, and never for quenching thirst; water, the totally nonfattening drink, is the chosen beverage for thirsty dieters.

Educational programs at NIF include lectures by Sorenson and other speakers and food preparation demonstrations twice a week by Gifford. Overfat individuals are counseled to make good eating choices and to avoid sugar, salt, oil, and alcohol, when socializing or dining out. Evenings at the Institute are social times, without recreational eating and drinking; cultural events and facilities for other sports activities are close by.

The Institute's program provides a unique and affordable fitness education in wonderfully scenic surroundings—the view alone is worth it.

Bonaventure Resort Hotel and Spa

Guests at the Bonaventure Resort Hotel and Spa in Fort Lauderdale, Florida, are confronted with an unusual dilemma—with so many activities to select from each day, how does one choose? In addition to the par course and the sun decks, the saunas and the steam rooms, and the well-equipped gymnasiums, guests have access to a country club with two eighteen-hole championship courses, a racquet club where lessons are given by experts, a saddle club for riding and jumping horses, and the Town Center Club, which houses a roller skating rink, bowling alleys, and hobby rooms.

Water is everywhere—from the breathtaking fountains, the lake, and a manmade rain forest to the Swiss showers and pools—pools for exercising and swimming, whirlpools, and hot and cold plunge pools. Water is even used in a special Bonaventure wet massage designed by Lancôme to rid the skin of dead, dry cells. And guests are encouraged to drink lots of water—six to eight eight-ounce glasses a day.

The Bonaventure Fitness Program ranges from super-vised walks to weight training using barbells and Paramount equipment. Exercise schedules tailored to individual needs usually include some form of aerobics and are drawn up by the Bonaventure's trained fitness staff after consulting with each guest. Special programs for weight, cholesterol, and stress reduction have been designed to help harried execu-tives regain and maintain fitness and energy. Programs run for either four or seven days and include not only scheduled exercise but ample time for indulging in a favorite sport or for just relaxing.

One of the most pleasant aids to relaxation is massage, which can soothe muscles not used in exercise, release ten-sion caused by stress, and increase circulation and digestion. Both Swedish massage and Oriental massage are performed at the Bonaventure by trained masseurs. Shiatsu, the Oriental massage based on unblocking energy points through finger and hand pressure, is said to leave the massagee with a heightened sense of well-being.

Other roads to relaxation include facials and a wide range of beauty treatments (with Lancôme products) available in the beauty and barber shops. Guests can also browse in the boutiques, or try a herbal wrap in sheets permeated with the scents of hibiscus, chamomile, and peppermint. Swaddling in this delicious warmth in a darkened room, with cool cloths on forehead and throat, seems to melt away most tensions.

Exercise, of course, is only half of any weight control/fit-ness program. The other half is what the Bonaventure calls "Nutrition Life-Style." Besides the usual low-salt, low-sugar, low-fat meals common to weight-loss and good nutrition programs, the resort has assembled an assortment of ethnic meals to give guests a wider choice of food. Andrew Adri-ance, the spa's dietician, suggests using fresh fruits and vege-tables as snacks and consuming only half the entrée when eating out. He stresses eating three meals a day, meals high in fiber and complex carbohydrates (starch). Adriance has created recipes with a practical approach so that guests can continue the diet when they leave Bonaventure. Recipes from Canada to New Zealand include salads and soups to start each meal.

CANADIAN CUCUMBER SALAD WITH MINT AND SCALLIONS

3 medium-size cucumbers
1/2 cup sour cream
1 tablespoon finely minced fresh mint or 1 teaspoon dried
1 tablespoon raspberry vinegar
2 scallion tops, thinly sliced
1 teaspoon fructose
1/4 cup minced fresh parsley
1/2 teaspoon Veg-It seasoning (optional)

Peel cucumbers, then halve them lengthwise. Remove all seeds, then cut crosswise into thin crescents. Place in medium-size bowl. Combine remaining ingredients in a small bowl. Pour over cucumbers and toss to coat well. Cover and refrigerate at least 2 hours prior to serving.

SERVINGS: 4. CALORIES PER SERVING: 53

ENSALADA MALAGA

2 heads Bibb lettuce
2 cups fresh grapefruit sections
1/2 cup dry vermouth
1 cup low-fat cottage cheese
1/2 cup plain low-fat yogurt
2 tablespoons lemon juice

1/4 teaspoon cracked black pepper
1/4 cup chopped fresh chives
Garnish: Paprika

Separate lettuce leaves; wash and pat dry. Refrigerate. Pour vermouth over grapefruit sections in 2-cup glass measure. Refrigerate for at least 2 hours.

Meanwhile, purée cottage cheese with yogurt, lemon juice, and pepper in blender 1 1/2 to 2 minutes, or till smooth. Stir in chives and refrigerate.

Arrange 3 to 4 Bibb lettuce leaves flat on each of 6 salad plates, first removing any coarse white parts. Pour 1/4 cup of the cottage cheese dressing across the center of each of the lined plates. Drain vermouth from grapefruit sections and discard. Arrange 1/3 cup of grapefruit sections over salad dressing on each plate and sprinkle with dash of paprika. Serve immediately.

SERVINGS: 6. CALORIES PER SERVING: 48

GREEK EGG-LEMON SOUP

4 cups chicken stock
1 tablespoon cornstarch
1/4 cup cold water
2 egg whites
2 tablespoons lemon juice
1 teaspoon grated lemon zest
1/4 teaspoon freshly ground white pepper
Vege-It to taste (optional)

Bring chicken stock to a boil in a medium-size saucepan. Dissolve cornstarch in cold water. Add to stock and cook 2 to 3 minutes over medium heat till mixture begins to thicken. Beat egg whites till stiff peaks form; then add to stock slowly. Turn off heat immediately. Add lemon juice and zest, white pepper, and Vege-It (if desired). Serve hot in soup cups.

SERVINGS: 4. CALORIES PER SERVING: 21

NEW ZEALAND CURRIED CHICKEN SOUP

2 teaspoons corn oil margarine
3 tablespoons seasoned bread crumbs
1/2 teaspoon curry powder
3 cups chicken stock
1 cup skim milk
1/4 pound cooked white-meat chicken, finely shredded
Garnish: 2 teaspoons minced chives and freshly ground
    black pepper

Melt margarine in medium-size saucepan. Add bread crumbs and curry powder and sauté over medium heat 2 to 3 minutes, stirring frequently. Slowly add chicken stock and skim milk and continue stirring till mixture just begins to boil. Add chicken, reduce heat to low, and simmer 10 minutes. Pour into soup cups, garnish, and serve immediately.

SERVINGS: 4. CALORIES PER SERVING: 84

Entrées are primarily vegetarian, seafood, or light meat such as veal or poultry. No red meat is served, as it is high in fat and cholesterol content.

The beauty of the following soup is the colors and textures of the garnishes added to the soup as it is portioned into cups or small bowls. Sumashi is simply a clear soup stock. Bonaventure uses chicken stock, while genuine sumashi is made with dashi, a type of fish stock with MSG and high-sodium Japanese soy sauce added. Most fish stocks require sodium to mask their pronounced bitter taste.

JAPANESE SUMASHI

Sumashi:
6 cups chicken stock
1 tablespoon low-sodium soy sauce

Garnishes:
1 1/4-inch tofu cube
4 very thin carrot, zucchini, or celery strips
3 cooked kidney beans
1 thin lemon slice
1 small parsley sprig
5 1/2 pieces scallion tops
12 to 15 grains cooked rice or vermicelli pieces
5 watercress leaves
2 thin mushroom slices

Heat stock to a boil in a large saucepan. Meanwhile, prepare three contrasting garnishes from the list above (amounts are for 1 serving); arrange garnishes in individual bowls or cups. Stir soy sauce into soup, then carefully pour soup over garnishes and serve immediately.

SERVINGS: 6. CALORIES PER SERVING: 15

ORIENTAL TOFU BURGERS

1 pound firm tofu
1/2 cup whole-wheat bread crumbs
2 egg whites
1 whole egg
1/4 cup grated carrot
1/4 cup minced scallions
2 tablespoons toasted sesame seeds
1 tablespoon low-sodium soy sauce
1/4 teaspoon ground coriander
2 cloves garlic, crushed
1/4 cup diced celery
2 tablespoons Dijon mustard
1/4 cup diet catsup
Vegetable oil
Garnish: Sliced fresh, ripe tomatoes and lettuce leaves

Squeeze moisture from tofu and blot on paper toweling. Place in medium-size bowl and mash with fork until consistency of cottage cheese. Add all remaining ingredients except vegetable oil and garnishes and stir till well combined. Form mixture into 6 "burgers." Heat enough vegetable oil to cover pan till almost smoking in medium-size nonstick pan. Carefully place burgers in pan and cook over medium heat 5 minutes, then turn over and cook an additional 8 to 10 minutes, till lightly browned. Serve hot, garnished with sliced tomato and lettuce. Accompany with diet catsup, using about 2 teaspoons per burger.

SERVINGS: 6. CALORIES PER SERVING: 176

PETRALE SOLE EN PAPILLOTE

1 tablespoon corn oil margarine
1 tablespoon chopped shallots
1/3 cup dry vermouth
12 medium-size fresh mushrooms, finely chopped
Vegetable oil
2 sole fillets (5 ounces each)
6 thin lemon slices
Freshly ground black pepper to taste
Garnish: Lemon wedges and chopped fresh parsley

Preheat oven to 375 degrees.

Melt margarine in a small saucepan. Add shallots and sauté over medium heat till tender. Add vermouth and mushrooms, reduce heat to low, and cook, uncovered, until most of liquid has evaporated, 5 to 7 minutes. Set aside to cool.

Cut 2 pieces of parchment paper to the size of a 9-inch dinner plate; brush lightly with vegetable oil. Spread mushroom mixture over half of each piece of parchment paper, leaving a 1-inch border around edge. Place a sole fillet over each portion of mushroom mixture; arrange 3 lemon slices over each fillet and sprinkle with pepper to taste. Fold parchment paper over and secure edges by crimping. Place on a nonstick or lightly oiled cookie sheet and bake 20 minutes.

Serve as is, garnished with lemon wedges and fresh parsley.

SERVINGS: 2. CALORIES PER SERVING: 215

CODFISH ESPANA

2 codfish fillets (4 ounces each)
1/4 cup dry sherry or dry white wine
1/2 teaspoon grated fresh ginger
1 teaspoon corn oil
1 teaspoon finely chopped fresh chili
1/2 green bell pepper, seeded and diced
1/2 medium-size red bell pepper, seeded and diced
2 tablespoons diced onion
2 scallions, thinly sliced
1 cup tomato purée
1 1/2 teaspoons fennel leaves

Season codfish with sherry and ginger and let stand 20 minutes.

Heat corn oil in small skillet. Add all three peppers, onion, and scallions and sauté 3 to 4 minutes, till onion is transparent and peppers begin to soften. Add tomato purée and fennel leaves, stirring well to combine. Place codfish fillets in tomato mixture and baste well. Cover and simmer gently 10 to 12 minutes, or till fish is just cooked through. Test doneness by piercing center of a fillet with a fork; if center meat is white and has lost transparency, fish is done. Serve hot.

SERVINGS: 2. CALORIES PER SERVING: 220

SZECHUAN SQUID WITH VEGETABLES

1 pound cleaned small squid (1 1/2 pounds if not cleaned)
2 teaspoons cornstarch
3 tablespoons dry sherry
2 tablespoons plus 1 teaspoon peanut oil or corn oil
2 tablespoons grated fresh ginger

1 medium-size red bell pepper, seeded and diced
1 1/2 cups diagonally sliced (1/4 inch) celery
1 teaspoon finely diced fresh chili
3/4 cup bottled clam juice
1 tablespoon low-sodium soy sauce
6 scallions, sliced diagonally in 1/2-inch lengths
1/2 cup snow peas, trimmed

Rinse and drain cleaned squid. Cut bodies in half lengthwise, then crosswise into strips about 1/4 inch wide. Quarter or halve tentacles lengthwise.

Stir together cornstarch, sherry, and the 1 teaspoon peanut oil; combine with the squid and let marinate from 30 minutes to 2 hours, according to taste.

Heat the 2 tablespoons oil in large wok or skillet. Add the ginger, red pepper, snow peas, celery, and chili; stir-fry for 1 minute. Add clam juice and soy sauce and simmer 3 to 4 minutes, till celery is tender but still crisp. Add the squid with marinade, scallions, and snow peas. Cook 2 to 4 minutes, till squid is opaque and just firm. Serve immediately.

SERVINGS: 4. CALORIES PER SERVING: 215

BOLIVIAN ROAST VEAL

1 1/2 pounds boneless lean veal shoulder roast, rolled and
tied
2 cups water
1/2 teaspoon sea salt (optional)
2 teaspoons cider vinegar
1 bay leaf
1/2 teaspoon ground cumin
6 whole peppercorns
1 clove garlic, crushed
4 celery stalks, trimmed and sliced
1 medium-size fresh, ripe tomato, seeded and diced
1/2 cup coarsely diced carrot
1/2 small onion, chopped
1/2 teaspoon dried oregano
4 medium-size fresh apricots, pitted and halved, or 8
waterpack canned apricot halves
2 fresh plums or peaches, halved and pitted, or 4
waterpack canned halves of either

Preheat oven to 325 degrees.

Place meat in small roasting pan with water, salt (if
desired), vinegar, bay leaf, cumin, peppercorns, and garlic.
Cover loosely with foil and bake for 45 minutes. Remove
from oven, turn roast and baste. Add celery, tomato, carrot,
onion, oregano, and fruits to pan, cover and bake an additional 30 to 40 minutes, till vegetables are tender and internal temperature of meat reaches 155 degrees. Remove from
oven and let stand 15 minutes. Slice and serve with 1/2 cup
defatted roasting juices along with vegetables and fruits.

SERVINGS: 6. CALORIES PER SERVING: 185

VEAL MILANESE WITH ONIONS

4 veal scallops (3 1/2 ounces each)
1 egg, well beaten
1/4 cup low-fat milk
1/2 cup fresh bread crumbs
1/4 teaspoon dried oregano
1/2 teaspoon dried basil
1/2 teaspoon garlic powder
2 tablespoons olive oil
1/2 cup Chablis
1 large onion, coarsely chopped
1 cup beef stock
1 tablespoon lemon juice
1 teaspoon Worcestershire sauce

Flatten veal scallops to 1/4-inch thickness by lightly pounding with a meat mallet or rolling pin. In small bowl, mix together egg and milk. Spread bread crumbs on a piece of wax paper and combine with oregano, basil, and garlic powder. Dip veal into egg mixture, then dredge in bread crumb mixture.

Heat olive oil in medium-size nonstick skillet over medium-high heat. Sauté veal for 2 minutes on each side. Add wine to skillet; cook veal an additional 2 minutes, turning once. Remove veal to warm plate.

Add onion, beef stock, lemon juice, and Worcestershire sauce to pan drippings in skillet. Bring to boil over high heat and cook, uncovered, 3 to 4 minutes, till onions are soft and liquid has been slightly reduced. Serve veal immediately, with onion and sauce spooned over each portion.

SERVINGS: 4. CALORIES PER SERVING: 235

BREAD PUDDING WITH ORANGE SAUCE

2 eggs, well beaten
2 tablespoons fructose
1 teaspoon ground cinnamon
1/2 teaspoon freshly grated nutmeg
1/4 teaspoon ground cloves
1 teaspoon vanilla extract
2 tablespoons raisins
2 cups whole-wheat bread crumbs or 1 cup whole-wheat
    plus 1 cup white bread crumbs
1 cup hot skim milk
1/2 cup plus 6 tablespoons Orange Sauce (recipe follows)

Preheat oven to 350 degrees.

Combine eggs and fructose in bowl; blend in cinnamon, nutmeg, cloves, vanilla, and raisins. Add bread crumbs and milk and mix till combined. Pour the 1/2 cup orange sauce over mixture and stir 3 or 4 strokes, or just enough to marble sauce into mixture.

Pour batter into lightly oiled 9 × 5 × 3-inch loaf pan. Bake for 45 to 50 minutes, or till toothpick inserted in center comes out clean; be careful not to overbake.

To serve, slice pudding into 6 equal portions. Serve on flat plates, topping each portion with 1 tablespoon of orange sauce.

SERVINGS: 6. CALORIES PER SERVING: 99

ORANGE SAUCE

1 egg, beaten
1/3 cup fructose
Juice of 1 orange
Grated zest of 1 orange
1 teaspoon corn oil margarine

Combine egg, fructose, and orange juice and rind in a small saucepan. Add margarine and cook, stirring constantly, over low heat till thickened.

MAKES ABOUT 1 CUP. CALORIES PER TABLESPOON: 11

Note: Besides its use in the preceding recipe for Bread Pudding with Orange Sauce, this may also be used as a low-calorie syrup for crêpes or pancakes.

POACHED PEAR GLACÉ

2 ripe but firm pears
1 1/2 cups dry red wine
1 1/4 cups water
1 lemon, quartered
2 tablespoons fructose
1/2 teaspoon ground cinnamon
1 whole clove
1 tablespoon unflavored gelatin
Garnish: 4 lemon slices (cut and twisted) and fresh mint
   leaves

Peel pears and halve lengthwise. Remove core, but try to keep a piece of the stem attached to each half. Set aside.

Combine wine, 1 cup of the water, the lemon, fructose, and spices in a small saucepan; bring to a slow boil. Place pear halves, flat side down, in liquid; cover and cook over low heat 12 to 15 minutes, till pears are tender but not soft. Remove pears with slotted spoon to individual small bowls, one half pear per bowl, and refrigerate.

Soften gelatin in 1/4 cup cool water. Add to poaching liquid and bring to a boil. Remove from heat and let cool to room temperature.

Remove pears from refrigerator. With flat side down, make 6 or 8 lengthwise cuts from base of each pear three fourths of the way to the stem. Carefully curve out with hand to create a fanned look. Place pear halves back in small bowls, arranging them as you do so. Remove clove from poaching liquid and pour one fourth of liquid over each pear half. Chill at least 1 hour before serving.

To serve, garnish each pear half with a twisted lemon slice and mint leaves.

SERVINGS: 4. CALORIES PER SERVING: 52

GELATO

1 cup fructose
1 envelope unflavored gelatin
5 cups whole milk
3 eggs
2 teaspoons vanilla extract
Garnish: Fresh raspberries and mint leaves

Combine fructose and gelatin in a medium-size saucepan. Stir in 4 cups of the milk. Cook, stirring constantly, over medium heat till mixture reaches a slow boil. Remove from heat and set aside.

Beat eggs in a small bowl. Gradually stir 1 cup of the hot gelatin mixture into eggs. Stir egg mixture back into gelatin mixture. Stir over low heat till mixture thickens slightly. Stir in vanilla and remaining 1 cup milk. Freeze in ice cream freezer according to manufacturer's instructions.

To serve, scoop 1/2-cup portions into saucer champagne glasses. Garnish each serving with a fresh raspberry and mint leaves.

MAKES ABOUT 8 CUPS. CALORIES PER 1/2-CUP PORTION: 84

GLAZED FRUIT TART

1 envelope unflavored gelatin
1 cup unsweetened apple juice
1 tablespoon fructose

1 teaspoon lemon juice
12 kiwi slices (1/2 inch each)
16 banana slices (1/2 inch each)
8 large, fresh strawberries, halved lengthwise
Garnish: 4 fresh mint sprigs

Sprinkle gelatin over apple juice in a small saucepan and let soften. Bring mixture slowly to a boil, stirring frequently. Add fructose and lemon juice and cook an additional minute. Remove from heat and let cool to room temperature.

Meanwhile, layer fruit in each of four 4-ounce ramekins or small stemmed glasses as follows: Place 3 slices kiwi on bottom, followed by 4 slices banana, then 4 strawberry halves. Pour equal parts of cooled gelatin mixture over fruit and chill 2 to 3 hours, till firm.

Serve garnished with mint sprigs.

SERVINGS: 4. CALORIES PER SERVING: 65

BAKED APPLE WITH AMARETTO

2 baking apples, such as Jonathan or Golden Delicious
1/2 teaspoon cornstarch
1/4 cup water
1/2 cup apple juice
1/4 teaspoon ground allspice
1/2 teaspoon ground cinnamon
1 tablespoon Amaretto liqueur
2 tablespoons lemon juice
Garnish: 8 fresh mint leaves

Preheat oven to 375 degrees.

Halve apples, then remove core and stem, but do not peel. Place flat side down in small nonstick baking pan. Set aside.

Dissolve cornstarch in water in small saucepan; add apple juice, allspice, cinnamon, and Amaretto. Bring mixture to boil over medium heat, stirring frequently. Remove from heat and pour over apples. Cover with foil and bake for 40 minutes.

Cool 10 to 15 minutes before serving, or chill well. Serve in shallow glass bowls with natural juices poured over and garnished with 2 mint leaves apiece.

SERVINGS: 4. CALORIES PER SERVING: 54

STRAWBERRIES ROMANOFF

1 pint fresh strawberries, rinsed and halved, stems removed
3 tablespoons brandy
2 tablespoons Grand Marnier or other orange liqueur
1 teaspoon corn oil margarine
1 tablespoon grated orange zest
Pinch freshly grated nutmeg

Arrange strawberries in 4 saucer champagne glasses; refrigerate.

Combine remaining ingredients in a small saucepan. Cook over medium heat till mixture starts to simmer, about 1 minute. Remove from heat and carefully ignite with a long match. Shake pan well till flames subside, then spoon 1 tablespoon of mixture over each portion of strawberries.

Serve chilled.

SERVINGS: 4. CALORIES PER SERVING: 65

The "Nutrition Life-Style" diet is based on 900 calories a day and achieves its goal by controlling the size of portions. Guests are admonished to eat slowly, never while reading or watching TV, as eating should be enjoyed for its own sake. Decaffeinated coffee, herbal teas, and Postum are served with meals; alcohol is not permitted in the spa dining room.

In addition to spa facilities, the hotel has 600 guest rooms and suites in nine separate buildings (each with its own concierge) and a 35,000-square-foot World Conference Center with the latest in electronic systems and audiovisual equipment. Participants in the Spa Plan have their choice of any of the hotel social activities in the evening, or they can attend special programs ranging from discussions of "wellness" concepts to psychic demonstrations.

Transportation is available from both the Fort Lauderdale and Miami airports (both within twenty-five miles).

The Heartland

Gerald Kaufman and Charlotte Newberger believe that the Corn Belt should offer the same services available at Sun Belt resorts, which is why they purchased the Kam Lake Estate in Gilman, Illinois, eighty miles south of Chicago. The estate, on thirty-one acres of wooded land, includes a twenty-room mansion, a multilevel barn, and a three-acre manmade lake. After expensive and extensive renovations, the resort opened in November 1983 as a year-round fitness retreat for men and women.

The Heartland specializes in helping guests attain their health and fitness objectives in a friendly, supportive atmosphere. The moral support of working out and playing with others who share similar goals is an important part of The Heartland's philosophy; the overall objective of The Heartland is to provide guests with the information and skills needed to change and grow—to begin living in a healthy way.

Guests stay at the spacious Kam Lake mansion. The mansion/guest house, comfortable in all seasons, includes a library, lounges, wood-burning fireplaces, and a large dining room looking out onto Kam Lake. An underground passage connects the guest house with the converted barn/spa, which is equipped with an indoor pool, steam rooms and saunas, and all the latest high-tech exercise equipment. Aerobic exercises on rowing machines and stationary bicycles are alternated with weight training on pneumatic resistance machines or the "supercircuit" equipment. Gravity inversion equipment is available, and all guests are provided with respironic pulse monitors.

Outdoor athletic programs are geared to the seasons and include a wide spectrum of sports from swimming and tennis to cross-country skiing and ice skating. While the fitness programs are challenging and require a certain amount of hard work, the staff firmly believes in helping guests to enjoy themselves, to develop childlike spontaneity as an aid to healthy living. For those who think spas are for summer only, The Heartland notes that exercising in cold weather is actually advantageous, as the body then burns more fuel (fat).

Weight loss is not the primary purpose of the retreat's cuisine—eating sensibly is—but a low-calorie diet is available upon request. Because "we are what we eat," good nutrition is the basis for The Heartland's lifestyle-modification concept. The menus are largely vegetarian, supplemented with fish. Fresh, organically grown produce, obtained from a nearby farm whenever seasonally possible, is used for creating meals high in complex carbohydrates and fiber and low in fat and sodium.

Nutrition and cooking classes are offered but are only a part of The Heartland's educational program. Guests can participate in workshops on assertiveness training and techniques for dealing with stress, yoga and meditation classes are offered, and guest lecturers speak on topics ranging from acupuncture to neurolinguistic programming (the theory that you are not only just what you eat—you are also what you say).

Special holiday programs are available at reduced rates.

Roommates will be provided for single guests who desire double occupancy.

The Heartland also supplies exercise clothing, jackets and rainwear, and evening leisurewear for its guests. Massages, facials, and beauty treatments are available at no additional cost, as is, of course, use of all Heartland facilities.

Because enrollment for each session is limited, The Heartland's staff is able to give each guest the personal attention he or she needs to modify harmful habits and begin living a healthy life.

Susan Witz, director of Education and Nutrition, and her staff have created recipes with a sensible approach, recipes that use seasonally available and relatively inexpensive ingredients. Here are some of their ideas:

HEARTLAND MUFFINS

1 cup unprocessed bran
1 1/4 cups low-fat milk
4 tablespoons butter
1/3 cup honey
1/3 cup molasses
2 eggs, beaten
1 1/2 cups whole-wheat flour
2 1/4 teaspoons baking powder
1/4 cup raisins
1/4 cup chopped walnuts

Preheat oven to 400 degrees.

Combine bran and milk. Let stand 10 minutes.

Cream butter with honey, then beat in molasses and eggs. Add to bran mixture. Combine dry ingredients in separate bowl. Add to batter a third at a time, taking care not to overmix. Bake in oiled muffin tins for 20 to 30 minutes.

MAKES 15 MUFFINS. CALORIES PER MUFFIN: 75

YOGURT WITH HAZELNUTS AND HONEY

3 tablespoons hazelnuts
2 cups plain low-fat yogurt
1/2 teaspoon grated lemon or orange zest
Freshly grated nutmeg to taste
1 tablespoon honey

Preheat oven to 350 degrees.

Roast hazelnuts till skins blister, 10 to 15 minutes. Set them in a dish towel for a minute, then rub vigorously to remove skins. Chop coarsely. Stir zest gently into yogurt and spoon into 6 serving bowls. Distribute nuts over yogurt, grate nutmeg over each, and drizzle on honey to finish.

SERVINGS: 6. CALORIES PER SERVING: 80

CORN, OAT, AND BERRY MUFFINS

1 1/4 cups low-fat milk
1 egg, beaten
2 tablespoons honey
3 tablespoons melted butter or oil
1 cup whole-wheat pastry flour
1/2 cup cornmeal
1/2 cup ground rolled oats (use food processor or
     blender to reduce to a fine flake)
3 teaspoons baking powder
1/2 cup frozen raspberries or blueberries, thawed

Preheat oven to 425 degrees.

Whisk liquid ingredients together. Combine dry ingredients in a separate bowl. Quickly combine the two, stirring in berries. Turn into oiled muffin tins and bake for about 20 minutes, till muffins are golden on top.

MAKES 12 MUFFINS. CALORIES PER MUFFIN: 120

STUFFED POTATOES

2 large baking potatoes
1 cup cottage cheese
1/4 cup freshly grated Parmesan cheese
1/2 cup grated mozzarella cheese
2 tablespoons chopped fresh parsley
2 tablespoons chopped fresh dill
Freshly ground black pepper to taste

Preheat oven to 350 degrees. Bake potatoes in aluminum foil for 1 hour, or till tender. Remove potatoes from oven and cut in half lengthwise; leave oven on at 350 degrees. Carefully scoop out flesh from potato skin into bowl. Stir in remaining ingredients, mixing well. Spoon filling back into skins and bake at 350 degrees 15 minutes, or till filling is browned.

SERVINGS: 4. CALORIES PER SERVING: 145

VEGETABLE PÂTÉ

3 cups broccoli florets, steamed
6 eggs
1 cup whole-wheat flour
2 tablespoons dried basil
2 teaspoons freshly ground black pepper
3 cups cauliflower florets, steamed
1/3 cup unbleached white flour
2 tablespoons ground coriander
1/2 teaspoon salt
3 cups peeled and chopped carrots, steamed
2 teaspoons mace or nutmeg
2 tablespoons honey, if carrots are bland

Purée broccoli in food processor. Add 2 of the eggs, 1/2 cup of the whole-wheat flour, the basil, and black pepper; blend thoroughly, then remove mixture from processor and set aside.

Purée cauliflower in food processor. Add 2 of the eggs, the white flour, coriander, and salt; blend thoroughly, then remove mixture from processor and set aside.

Purée carrots in food processor. Add 2 remaining eggs, remaining flour, mace or nutmeg, and honey, if desired. Blend thoroughly.

Preheat oven to 350°.

Lightly butter a 3 × 3 × 14-inch loaf pan. Line pan with wax paper; lightly butter paper. Carefully layer the broccoli, cauliflower, and carrot mixtures, making sure to distribute each mixture evenly about the pan before pouring the next in.

Place loaf pan in larger pan filled with 3 to 4 inches of boiling water. Cover, if possible, leaving 1 to 1 1/2 inches for the pâté to rise. Place in oven and bake for 1 1/2 hours.

When done, remove loaf pan from water, allow to cool, then refrigerate for at least 3 hours or overnight.

When ready to serve, take a knife and loosen the pâté from the sides of the pan, invert, and remove pâté. Slice and serve with the following accompaniments:

Lettuce leaves
Whole-wheat bread
Sliced tomatoes
Sliced onions
Dijon mustard

MAKES 1 LOAF. CALORIES PER 4-TABLESPOON SERVING: 65.

COTTAGE CHEESE-HERB DIP

2 cups low-fat cottage cheese
3 tablespoons minced scallions
1/4 cup minced fresh parsley
1/4 cup minced fresh dill
1/4 cup minced pimiento
Freshly ground black pepper to taste

Combine all ingredients and mix well. Serve with fresh-cut vegetables or layered with Vegetable Pâté (see preceding recipe).

MAKES ABOUT 3 CUPS. CALORIES PER TABLESPOON: 10

STUFFED MUSHROOMS

1 cup cottage cheese
1/2 cup ricotta cheese
1/2 cup grated mozzarella cheese
1/2 cup chopped fresh spinach
1/4 cup minced scallions
1/4 teaspoon freshly grated nutmeg
Pinch freshly ground white pepper
24 large, fresh mushrooms, stems removed

Preheat oven to 350 degrees.

Combine cheeses with the spinach, scallions, nutmeg, and pepper; mix well. Fill mushroom caps with mixture. Bake on a greased baking sheet for 25 minutes. Serve immediately.

SERVINGS: 6. CALORIES PER SERVING: 160

JAPANESE MUSHROOM SALAD

1 cup sliced fresh mushrooms
2 tablespoons diced red bell pepper
1 tablespoon chopped fresh parsley or coriander (cilantro)
1 tablespoon diagonally cut scallion
2 tablespoons rice vinegar
1 teaspoon lime or lemon juice
1/2 teaspoon sesame-seed or other oil
Freshly ground black pepper to taste
Ground coriander to taste
Garnish: 1 teaspoon roasted hulled sesame seeds and 1
    lime wedge

Combine mushrooms, red pepper, parsley, and scallion in
salad bowl. Mix vinegar, juice, oil, pepper, and coriander;
pour dressing over vegetables and toss. Garnish with seeds
and lime wedge and serve.
    SERVINGS: 2. CALORIES PER SERVING: 40

PINK GRAPEFRUIT AND AVOCADO SALAD
WITH HONEY-POPPYSEED DRESSING

3 pink grapefruit, peeled
2 avocados
1/2 teaspoon Dijon mustard
1 teaspoon honey
1 teaspoon lime or lemon juice, or to taste
1 tablespoon almond or other oil
1 tablespoon poppyseeds, warmed in oven before adding
Freshly ground black pepper to taste
Red leaf or other lettuce

Using a sharp knife, section grapefruit into a bowl to catch
the juices. Chill for at least 1 hour. Peel, seed, and halve

avocados. Cut avocado halves into thin crescent slices. Remove grapefruit from bowl with slotted spoon. Mound grapefruit and avocado on beds of lettuce on 6 individual salad plates. Whisk remaining ingredients into grapefruit juice in bowl. Season with more lime or lemon juice and pepper, if desired, and spoon dressing over salads.

SERVINGS: 6. CALORIES PER SERVING: 150

APPLE-ENDIVE SLAW WITH BUTTERMILK DRESSING

4 radishes, sliced
3 apples, cored, quartered, and sliced crosswise
1 cup slivered Chinese or green cabbage
3 Belgian endives, cored and sliced crosswise
1/4 cup chopped toasted walnuts
2 egg yolks
1/2 cup buttermilk
3 tablespoons walnut, almond, or other oil
1 tablespoon cider vinegar
1 tablespoon lemon juice
2 teaspoons Dijon mustard
1 teaspoon grated lemon zest (optional)
1 teaspoon ground coriander or dill seeds
Freshly ground black pepper to taste
Lettuce leaves
Garnish: 3 tablespoons pomegranate seeds or celery
    leaves

Combine radishes, apples, cabbage, endives, and walnuts in salad bowl. Whisk together egg yolks, buttermilk, oil, vinegar, lemon juice, mustard, lemon zest, coriander, and pepper. Pour dressing over salad, toss, and chill thoroughly.

To serve, divide salad among 6 individual salad plates lined with lettuce leaves. Top with pomegranate and/or celery leaves.

SERVINGS: 6. CALORIES PER SERVING: 175

MEXICAN SQUASH SOUP

2 butternut squash, peeled, seeded, and cubed
1 bay leaf
2 cups vegetable stock or water
2 tablespoons vegetable oil
1 cup chopped onion
2/3 cup chopped celery root or celery
1 tablespoon ground coriander
1 teaspoon ground cumin
1 large clove garlic, minced
Freshly ground black pepper to taste
Garnish: Chopped celery leaves, roasted pumpkin seeds, blanched fresh corn kernels, or finely chopped red bell pepper.

Simmer squash and bay leaf in stock in a large saucepan till soft. Heat oil in skillet and sauté onion, celery, coriander, and cumin till vegetables are soft and fragrant. Add garlic and stir, then add vegetable mixture to squash-stock mixture. Heat together a few minutes. Remove bay leaf.

Purée mixture in a food processor or food mill. Return to saucepan and heat to serving temperature. Add pepper to taste and serve, garnished as desired.

SERVINGS: 6. CALORIES PER SERVING: 70

PERUVIAN FISH STEW

2 tablespoons olive oil
2 large onions, finely chopped
1 teaspoon crushed red pepper
2 large cloves garlic, pressed
4 large fresh, ripe tomatoes, peeled, seeded, and cut into
    bite-size chunks
1/4 cup tomato paste
4 tablespoons uncooked brown rice
2 1/2 quarts vegetable stock
4 pounds fish fillets, skinned and cut into 1 1/2-inch
    chunks
1 cup coarsely chopped red bell pepper
16 small red potatoes, cooked
Kernels from 5 ears corn
2 cups frozen peas
2 small bay leaves
1 teaspoon dried marjoram

Heat oil in a large saucepan. Add onion, crushed red pepper, garlic, tomatoes, tomato paste, and rice (in that order). Stir and cook for a few minutes, then add boiling stock. Bring to a boil, then lower heat and simmer 15 minutes. Add fish and simmer 5 more minutes. Add remaining ingredients and allow stew to simmer an additional 5 minutes.

SERVINGS: 10. CALORIES PER SERVING: 490

GRILLED SWORDFISH WITH ROSEMARY

6 swordfish steaks, each 1 inch thick
1/3 cup olive oil
1/4 cup lemon juice
2 cloves garlic, crushed

1 tablespoon finely chopped fresh rosemary or 2
    teaspoons dried
Freshly ground black pepper to taste
Garnish: Lemon wedges

Prepare charcoal to grill fish (using mesquite for flavor) or
preheat broiler.
    Rub fish with lemon juice, crushed garlic, and olive oil.
Then press rosemary into both sides of fish, and grind pepper
over to taste. Grill till fish is just cooked through, turning
once. If coal-grilling, guard from cooking over too hot coals;
if broiling, cook about 6 inches from heat source. Serve
immediately, with lemon wedges.
    SERVINGS: 6. CALORIES PER SERVING: 380

INDONESIAN FISH AND VEGETABLE BROCHETTES

Marinade:
2 tablespoons Thai chili paste with bean oil (see note below)
1/4 cup sesame-seed oil
2 tablespoons roasted sesame-seed oil (see note below)
2 tablespoons honey or brown sugar, firmly packed
2 to 3 tablespoons grated fresh ginger
1/3 cup lime juice
2 large cloves garlic, minced
1 tablespoon soy sauce
1 tablespoon ground coriander
1 teaspoon dried basil
1 tablespoon grated lime zest (optional)

Fish:
2 pounds swordfish or marlin, cut in 1 1/2-inch cubes

Vegetables:
(Choose from these to total about 9 cups)
Whole cherry tomatoes
Red onion, cut to skewer size
Red or green bell pepper, cut to skewer size
Whole mushrooms
Garnish: lime wedges and 3 tablespoons chopped peanuts

Mix marinade early so flavors have time to blend. Place fish in marinade and set aside for 1 to 2 hours.

Prepare grill or broiler. Skewer vegetables for 6 plates, alternating ingredients for color; cherry tomatoes are best skewered alone, as they are quick-cooking. Drain fish and skewer, alternating with red onion. Brush remaining marinade onto vegetable skewers.

When coals are at a slow, hot glow (or broiler is hot), grill vegetables (about 8 to 10 minutes), fish and onion (about 5 minutes), and cherry tomatoes (2 to 3 minutes).

Serve immediately, accompanied by lime wedges, topping the fish with chopped peanuts.

SERVINGS: 6. CALORIES PER SERVING: 315

Note: Available in Thai/Indonesian or other Oriental markets. If the chili paste with bean oil is not available, substitute 1/2 to 1 teaspoon chili powder, 1 tablespoon miso, and 1 tablespoon soy sauce.

HEARTLAND PUMPERNICKEL BREAD

1 tablespoon active dry yeast
1/4 cup lukewarm water
2 tablespoons safflower oil
1 tablespoon caraway seeds
2 tablespoons grated lemon zest
1 1/2 tablespoons carob powder
2 tablespoons molasses
1/3 cup dried currants

2 cups low-fat milk
2 1/2 cups rye flour
3 1/2 cups whole-wheat flour
1 cup unprocessed bran
1/2 cup wheat germ
1/2 cup gluten flour
1/2 cup soaked rye berries

Dissolve yeast in water in small bowl. Combine oil, caraway seeds, lemon peel, carob powder, molasses, currants, and low-fat milk in a large mixing bowl. Add yeast mixture, then stir in rye flour and half of whole-wheat flour, 1 cup at a time. Stir till smooth. Add bran, wheat germ, gluten flour, and rye berries; mix well.

Place dough on floured board, knead in remaining whole-wheat flour. Knead till smooth and elastic, then form into a ball. Place in an oiled bowl, cover with a damp towel, and let rise till doubled in bulk, an hour or more.

Punch dough down and form into 2 round loaves. Place loaves far apart on a greased large baking sheet. Let rise till almost doubled. Preheat oven to 375 degrees. Brush loaves with cold water and bake for 50 minutes.

Remove to racks to cool completely before serving.

MAKES 2 ROUND LOAVES. CALORIES PER LOAF: 1,000

WINTER RASPBERRY SORBET

3 ripe pears, peeled, cored, and chopped
3 tablespoons apple, cherry, or berry juice
2 cups frozen raspberries, thawed
2 teaspoons lemon juice, or to taste
Optional garnish: Tangerine, kiwi, or lime slices

Poach pears in juice in small saucepan till soft. Add to frozen raspberries in food processor and purée until smooth. Add lemon juice to taste. Freeze mixture in an ice cream maker following manufacturer's directions. Turn into a metal bowl, cover, and cure in freezer for 2 hours but not any longer, or sorbet will become too hard (see note below).

Serve in stemmed dessert glasses, garnished with tangerine, kiwi, or lime slices for color, if desired.

SERVINGS: 6. CALORIES PER SERVING: 110

Note: If this happens, process in a food processor to soften and break sorbet up.

TANGERINE SORBET

1 tablespoon grated tangerine zest (removed before juicing)
1 quart freshly squeezed tangerine juice
1 tablespoon honey
2 tablespoons lime juice

Combine all ingredients. Freeze in an ice cream maker, following manufacturer's directions. Turn into a metal bowl when frozen, cover, and cure in freezer for 2 hours but not any longer, or sorbet will become too hard (see note above in preceding recipe). Serve with Winter Raspberry Sorbet in a stem glass with garnish.

SERVINGS: 6. CALORIES PER SERVING: 90

Note: If desired, you can turn this into a party dessert by layering it with Winter Raspberry Sorbet (see preceding recipe) in stemmed dessert glasses and garnishing with fruit slices.

SERVINGS: 12. CALORIES PER SERVING: 100

The Oaks/The Palms

W omen over forty, traditionally considered the best candidates for "fat farms," have a fantastic role model in Sheila Cluff, founder/owner of two resort hotels —The Oaks at Ojai and The Palms at Palm Springs. Canadian-born Cluff, a former championship skater, first became interested in weight control during her somewhat sedentary college days when her weight reached a record 140 pounds, plump for her five-feet, four-inch frame. Today she is a size six.

As an athlete Cluff has always been fitness conscious. This interest, combined with a keen business acumen inherited from her successful father and enhanced by lots of energy and drive, have enabled Cluff to become the versatile success she is today—mother of four, community and business leader, renowned lecturer.

She is listed in *Who's Who of American Women,* has written a best-selling book called *Sheila Can Show You How,* arranges fitness cruises and tours, and now co-hosts a daily fitness show on ABC television. The show focuses on different body areas each day and emphasizes the importance of warming up, aerobics, and stretching/flexibility exercises. Her theories on the value of exercise are the cornerstone of the philosophy of her two health and fitness spas.

Before opening her spas, Cluff taught fitness classes for the Oxnard Parks and Recreation Department. She then became fitness director at The Oaks, which she subsequently purchased; later she acquired a second spa, The Palms. At the resorts she teaches guests how to buy, cook, and eat for health, in addition to directing the fitness programs. The atmosphere is low key. Guests are encouraged but not required to participate in any of the twelve exercise classes offered daily.

Some of Cluff's tips for lifelong fitness are: first, to find an exercise program that is appealing and enjoyable, and second, to practice this program at least three times a week. Pool exercises, in particular, are beneficial because 82 percent of one's body weight is "lost" when immersed in water and water gives one a freer range of motion. Also, water, like exercise itself, is a natural tranquilizer. Cluff believes there is a definite relationship between physical exercise and the ability to use mental capacities completely.

Guests at the two spas enjoy a brisk or moderate pace in their one- to three-mile pre-breakfast walk. Breakfasts are light, as a prelude to the difficult aerobics class that follows. Typical breakfast fare is a small piece of fruit, a packet of vitamins and minerals designed especially for the resorts by a biochemist, and a muffin, sans butter.

THE ORANGE-OAT MUFFIN

3 cups rolled oats
1/4 cup rice flour
1/8 teaspoon ground coriander
3/4 cup orange juice
2 eggs
1 cup sliced carrots
1 teaspoon vanilla extract
1/2 cup pitted dates

Preheat oven to 350 degrees. Spray 24 muffin cups with low-fat vegetable coating.

Combine oats, rice flour, and coriander in large bowl and set aside. Combine orange juice, eggs, and carrots in blender. Process till carrots are finely chopped. Add vanilla and dates. Process again till dates are finely chopped.

Fold contents of blender into dry ingredients. Spoon a heaping tablespoonful of batter into each prepared muffin cup. Bake for 45 minutes.

MAKES 24 MUFFINS. CALORIES PER MUFFIN: 65

Note: A perfect muffin for those allergic to wheat or milk products.

The Fitness Nutrition Plan at the spas is based on approximately 750 calories a day, although "man-sized" portions are available for nondieters. Average weight loss is a pound per day. Lunches and dinners are three-course meals—soup or salad, entree (which may also be a salad), and fruit or dessert. Soup stocks, always on hand in the resorts' kitchens and freezers, are used to prepare a variety of low-calories dishes.

STOCK

Save all bones, meat scraps, leftover vegetables, and vegeta-
    ble parings in a 3-quart soup kettle in the refrigerator till
    it's half to three-fourths full
1 medium-size onion
1 clove garlic
1 bay leaf
1 tablespoon kelp
3 peppercorns

Combine all ingredients in stock pot. Cover with boiling
water (sprout water if available) and simmer, uncovered, 3
hours. Cool, skim off fat, and strain. Use as base for soups.
Stock may also be made with only vegetables.
    YIELD DEPENDENT ON SIZE OF STOCK POT. CALORIES PER
SERVING: NEGLIGIBLE

OAKS ONION SOUP

5 medium-size onions, thinly sliced
6 tablespoons beef bouillon or soup stock
6 cups boiling water
1 tablespoon soy sauce
Garnish: 2 tablespoons freshly grated Parmesan cheese

Combine all the ingredients except the cheese in a saucepan.
Simmer 30 minutes. Sprinkle 1 teaspoon Parmesan cheese
on each serving.
    SERVING: 6. CALORIES PER SERVING: 40

BASIC BLENDER BROCCOLI SOUP

2 cups chicken stock
2 cups chopped broccoli

Combine ingredients in a saucepan and bring to a boil. Remove from heat; purée in blender. Reheat or serve chilled.

SERVINGS: 6. CALORIES PER SERVING: 14

Eleanor Brown, the spas' district manager in charge of food, has over twenty years' experience in gourmet cooking using natural foods, and is a member of the American Nutritional Consultant's Association. As an aid to preparing delicious, low-calorie recipes she substitutes blackstrap molasses, half quantities of honey, and fruits for sugar. She replaces white flour with whole wheat (3/4 cup whole-wheat flour = 1 cup white) and suggests sweetening tea and coffee with cinnamon. Her formulas for butter, sour cream, mayonnaise, dip, and sauces add richness to recipes without adding calories.

SUPER LOW-CAL BUTTER

1 stick soft sweet butter or 1 stick soft margarine
1/2 cup buttermilk

Place butter or margarine in glass 4-cup measuring cup. Whip till creamy with electric mixer. Add buttermilk and continue whipping slowly; the mixture will triple in volume.

MAKES ABOUT 3 CUPS. CALORIES PER TABLESPOON: 35

DELICIOUS LOW-CAL "SOUR CREAM"

1 cup low-fat cottage cheese
1/4 to 1/2 cup buttermilk
1/2 teaspoon lemon juice

Place ingredients in blender and blend till smooth and creamy.

MAKES 2 CUPS. CALORIES PER SERVING: 15

Note: At the Oaks, this is used as a dessert topping or base for salad dressing—very good, high in protein and low in fat.

Variation: For a creamy mayonnaise, add a little safflower oil.

CURRY DIP

2 cups low-fat cottage cheese
1/2 teaspoon curry powder
1/2 teaspoon dry mustard
1/2 teaspoon garlic powder
1/2 teaspoon prepared horseradish
1/2 teaspoon prepared mustard
1/2 teaspoon red wine vinegar
1/2 teaspoon grated onion

Combine all ingredients. Serve as a dip with vegetables.

MAKES 2 CUPS. CALORIES PER TABLESPOON: 15 TO 20

LEMON SAUCE FOR COOKED VEGETABLES

1 egg
1 1/3 cups low-fat cottage cheese

2 teaspoons red wine vinegar
1/4 cup lemon juice
1 tablespoon chopped fresh chives
2 teaspoons chopped fresh parsley
1 small clove garlic
Pinch dry mustard
1 tablespoon safflower oil

Blend all ingredients except oil till smooth in blender or food processor. Add oil as blender runs. Serve over cooked vegetables (absolutely delicious on broccoli, asparagus, artichokes, or cauliflower).

MAKES ABOUT 2 CUPS. CALORIES PER TABLESPOON: 20

THREE CHEESE CRÊPES

2 cups low-fat cottage cheese
1/4 cup grated mozzarella cheese
2 tablespoons grated onion
1/4 cup chopped fresh parsley
6 Creative Crêpes (recipe follows)
2 tablespoons grated Parmesan cheese

Preheat oven to 350 degrees. Combine cottage cheese, mozzarella, onion, and parsley in bowl; divide mixture evenly among the 6 crêpes. Roll up and place on baking pan or dish. Sprinkle each crêpe with 1 teaspoon of the Parmesan cheese. Bake for 20 minutes, or till brown.

SERVINGS: 6. CALORIES PER SERVING: 150

Note: A favorite with the guests at The Oaks. Add a little tomato sauce and you'll have mock cannelloni.

CREATIVE CRÊPES

2 eggs
1/3 cup non-instant nonfat dry milk
1/4 cup water

Combine ingredients in blender; blend. Cook like pancakes
in small crêpe pan sprayed with low-calorie vegetable coat-
ing.
  SERVINGS: 6. CALORIES PER SERVING: 45
  Note: These are high in protein and low in carbohydrates.
Be creative by varying fillings and toppings or serving as
French pancakes (with fresh fruit).

HOT TURKEY OR CHICKEN SALAD

2 cups diced, cooked chicken or turkey
2 cups diced celery
1/4 cup diced jícama
2 teaspoons grated onion
1 teaspoon soy sauce
1/4 cup Delicious Low-Cal Mayonnaise (see variation,
    page 154)
Grated cheddar cheese to taste

Preheat oven to 450 degrees.
  Combine chicken, vegetables, soy sauce, and mayonnaise
and spoon lightly into a baking dish. Sprinkle grated cheddar
cheese on top. Bake for 10 to 15 minutes, or till top is
browned.
  SERVINGS: 6. CALORIES PER SERVING: 149

WINNER'S RATATOUILLE

2 cups cubed yellow squash
2 teaspoons garlic powder
2 cups cubed eggplant
1/2 teaspoon dried oregano
3 medium-size onions, sliced
2 medium-size green bell peppers, sliced
1 teaspoon dried marjoram
4 medium-size fresh, ripe tomatoes, sliced
1 teaspoon dried basil

Preheat oven to 350 degrees.
    Place squash in baking pan. Add 1 teaspoon of the garlic
powder. Cover squash with eggplant. Sprinkle with oregano
and 1/2 teaspoon of the garlic powder. Layer onions and
peppers on eggplant. Sprinkle with marjoram and remaining
1/2 teaspoon garlic powder. Cover and bake for 35 minutes.
Add tomatoes and basil and bake, covered, for 10 more
minutes.
    SERVINGS: 10. CALORIES PER SERVING: 49

VEAL BURGUNDY

10 small or 5 medium-size onions, sliced
1 teaspoon beef bouillon
2 pounds boneless veal, cubed
Pinch each of freshly ground black pepper, dried
    marjoram, and dried thyme
1/2 cup water
1 cup burgundy wine
8 ounces fresh mushrooms, sliced

Sauté onions with the bouillon, in a frying pan over medium
heat, stirring constantly, till onion is translucent, almost 5

minutes. Remove from pan to separate dish. Brown veal on all sides in same pan. Sprinkle with seasonings, then add water and wine and simmer slowly, covered, for 3 1/2 to 4 hours. Cool meat, then chill in skillet.

Remove fat from meat, then return to low heat. Add mushrooms and sautéed onions; cook, covered, 1 hour longer.

SERVINGS: 8. CALORIES PER SERVING: 162

SKEWERED SCALLOPS

1/2 cup teriyaki sauce
1/2 cup unsweetened pineapple juice
Pinch dried dillweed
2 pounds sea scallops
6 large fresh mushrooms, cut in half
1 green bell pepper, seeded and cut in large pieces

Combine teriyaki sauce, pineapple juice, and dillweed in shallow glass dish. Alternate scallops, mushrooms, peppers on skewer. Marinate in teriyaki-pineapple juice mixture for 1 hour, turning occasionally. Preheat oven to 400 degrees. Drain kebabs and bake for 15–20 minutes. Serve immediately.

MAKES 6 KEBABS. CALORIES PER SERVING: 110

Note: Kebabs may also be barbecued over coals.

Variation: This is also good with shrimp or a combination of shrimp and scallops. You can also add other vegetables to the skewers.

EGG FOO YUNG (AND SLENDER)

2 scallions, finely chopped
1 green bell pepper, seeded and finely
    chopped

2 cups fresh bean sprouts
1 tablespoon soy sauce
4 eggs, beaten

Combine all ingredients well in a medium-size bowl. Drop
by spoonfuls onto a hot griddle sprayed with low-calorie
vegetable coating; cook till brown on both sides. Serve immediately.

SERVINGS: 6. CALORIES PER SERVING: 67
Note: You can vary the vegetables in this. Mushrooms and
water chestnuts are nice additions.

VERY POPULAR NO-PASTA LASAGNA

1/2 cup dry red wine
5 pitted olives, minced
2 cups tomato juice
1 medium-size onion, chopped
1 teaspoon each dried oregano, basil, and freshly ground
    black pepper
2 1/2 cups low-fat cottage cheese
1/2 cup grated mozzarella cheese
2 eggs
1/4 cup chopped fresh parsley
1/2 cup chopped scallions
1 large eggplant, thinly sliced
2 to 3 zucchini, thinly sliced lengthwise
1/4 cup freshly grated Parmesan cheese

Combine wine, olives, tomato juice, onion, green pepper,
and seasonings in a saucepan. Simmer, covered, 2 to 3 hours.
    Combine cottage cheese, mozzarella, eggs, parsley, and
scallions in a bowl. Mix well.
    Preheat oven to 350 degrees.
    Spray a lasagne pan or similar baking dish with low-fat
vegetable coating. Arrange a layer of half the eggplant slices

over bottom of pan and spoon over a third of the sauce. Spread half the cottage cheese filling over the sauce. Arrange all the zucchini slices over filling, top with half the remaining sauce, then the remaining filling. Cover filling with a layer of the remaining eggplant slices; top with remaining sauce and sprinkle the Parmesan over all. Bake for 1 hour.

Let stand for 10 minutes before serving.

SERVINGS: 6. CALORIES PER SERVING: 157

CHICKEN CHOP SUEY

1 tablespoon arrowroot
1/3 cup water
1 tablespoon safflower oil
2 cups chopped celery
2 cups bean sprouts
2 cups shredded cabbage
1/2 cup diced jícama
1/4 cup sliced onion
1 teaspoon crushed garlic
1 teaspoon crushed fresh ginger
2 tablespoons soy sauce
2 cups sliced fresh mushrooms
1 cup snow peas
2 cups cooked, shredded chicken

Dissolve arrowroot in water and set aside.

Heat oil in a wok or large skillet over high heat. Add celery, bean sprouts, cabbage, green pepper, jícama, onion, garlic, and ginger; stir-fry for 3 minutes. Add 1 tablespoon of the soy sauce, cover, and cook 3 minutes. Uncover and add mushrooms, snow peas, and chicken; stir till heated through. Add remaining 1 tablespoon soy sauce and arrowroot mixture; stir till thickened. Remove from heat and serve immediately.

SERVINGS: 6. CALORIES PER SERVING: 95

FITNESS FLAN

2 eggs
2 cups skim milk
2 tablespoons honey
Pinch freshly grated nutmeg
1 teaspoon vanilla extract

Preheat oven to 350 degrees.

Beat all ingredients in mixing bowl till creamy. Divide among 6 custard cups; stand cups in shallow pan with 1/2 inch water in bottom. Cover with foil; bake 20 to 25 minutes.

SERVINGS: 6. CALORIES PER SERVING: 80

Note: Use this for dessert when you are a little low on protein in the rest of the meal.

ORANGE "ZABAGLIONE"

1 envelope unflavored gelatin
1 1/4 cups orange juice
1 whole orange, cut up
1 teaspoon grated lemon zest
1 teaspoon vanilla extract
1/4 cup non-instant nonfat dry milk
2 ice cubes

Sprinkle gelatin over 1/4 cup orange juice in small saucepan and let soak for 5 minutes. Stir over low heat till gelatin is completely dissolved. Purée remaining orange juice, orange pieces, lemon zest, and vanilla in blender. Add powdered milk and ice cubes as mixture whips.

Stir in dissolved gelatin, then divide among 8 dessert dishes. Chill until set.

SERVINGS: 8. CALORIES PER SERVING: 40

Note: A nice light dessert. The Oaks ends its Italian meals with this.

SHEILA'S "CHEESECAKE" SUPREME

2 eggs
2 cups low-fat cottage cheese
2 tablespoons honey
2 teaspoons vanilla extract
1 teaspoon almond extract
2 tablespoons lemon juice
2 tablespoons non-instant nonfat dry milk

Preheat oven to 300 degrees.
    Combine all ingredients in blender and blend till creamy. Pour into a baking dish and bake for 30 minutes, or just till set. Set dish in a pan of water to cool slowly. Chill overnight.
    SERVINGS: 8. CALORIES PER SERVING: 100

The city of Ojai, about eighty minutes away from Los Angeles, is well known as an art colony. Set in a grove of oak trees, The Oaks is situated across the street from a beautiful park that hosts music and dance festivals and other cultural events. Golf, tennis, and other activities are available in the area, as are water sports on nearby Lake Casitas. Amenities include a grand gathering room, the Winner's Circle, where guests can hear lectures, play bridge or backgammon, or just relax. The less formal Garden Room, where bathing suits and gym clothes are acceptable attire, is just off the swimming pool and carpeted gym. Accommodations in either the separate or main lodge rooms are air conditioned and include color television sets.

    The Palms is close to downtown Palm Springs, a less than two-hour drive from Los Angeles. The setting is conducive to relaxation—orange trees, peaceful blue skies, and white Spanish-type buildings. A central lodge, cottages, and a multipurpose exercise building form a courtyard for the pool area. Golf courses, tennis courts, and all the attractions of

Palm Springs are nearby. Accommodations are similar to those at The Oaks. Guests at the resorts can arrange for massages, facials, or cellulite wraps.

The programs at both spas are coed. Although men make up only about 10 percent of the guest list (which has included Teri Garr, Magda Gabor, Shirley Jones, and June Allyson), men-only weekends are offered at The Oaks, and weight-training and exercise classes just for men are available three times a week at The Palms. Both resorts emphasize weight loss and fitness in a friendly, relaxed environment.

Four Seasons Hotel

In addition to the usual amenities of a quality metropolitan hotel, Philadelphia's Four Seasons Hotel now offers guests a two-day Revitalization Weekend. Check-in is Friday with the afternoon free for enjoying the city's rich historical heritage, shopping, or getting a head start on fitness in the hotel spa.

The hotel's location is ideal for walking, jogging, or running alongside the tree-lined Benjamin Franklin Parkway—past the Museum of Art to the East River Drive and through the park on the bank of the Schuylkill River.

Accommodations at the Four Seasons are first rate—377 spacious rooms and suites furnished with special amenities such as terry robes, hair dryers, remote-control televisions, and mini-bars. The goal is to offer a private and pleasant atmosphere in which guests are truly comfortable.

The same elegant ambiance prevails in the Four Seasons Hotel Spa where, amid flowers and foliage, guests will find a swimming pool, whirlpool, women's and men's saunas, and a massage room. Additional exercise equipment facilities include Universal equipment, treadmill, and stationary bicycles.

The Revitalization Weekend includes parking, deluxe accommodations for two nights, meals, and a number of optional classes ranging from light exercise to spirited workouts. Guests may participate in as few or as many as they like.

Guests stretch, breathe, and exercise in tandem with expert instructors. Lungs are cleansed by brisk morning walks; muscles are strengthened through aerobics. Moderately paced aquatic exercises in the indoor pool rejuvenate skin and surface muscles. Yoga relaxes and refreshes psyche and body. Dance routines are invigorating and fun. Body contouring warms and isolates muscle tone with instructed equipment use. There's also time for a facial and reflexology clinics, and a soothing and relaxing massage can be scheduled at the guest's convenience. There is also time to luxuriate in the whirlpool and saunas.

The revitalization program officially begins Friday at six with a crudités and mineral water reception, followed by dinner. The weekend includes six meals—lightly cooked, sugar free, and low in fat and sodium. Coffee (regular and decaffeinated), herbal teas, and mineral water are on hand all day; vegetable or fruit juices are brought to the guest's room soon after the 6:00 A.M. wake-up call and are also served at midmorning and after yoga classes.

Starting with wake-up stretches and a brisk three-mile pre-breakfast walk, several exercise classes led by trained instructors are scheduled for Saturday and Sunday. All activities are optional. Classes are limited to twenty participants, facilitating personal attention from the staff headed by Joanne Krantz, formerly with The Oaks at Ojai. More passive guests can indulge in a massage or learn how to give themselves a facial. Theaters, museums, and art galleries abound in the area, many within walking distance. The hotel's concierge keeps guests apprised of local entertainment and cultural events, and will make the necessary arrangements.

Breakfast is served in the Fountain Restaurant, lunch is poolside, and Saturday's dinner may be enjoyed in the Swann

Cafe or delivered to the room. Special spa recipes have been created for the program. Meals consist of lots of grains and greens, fruits and vegetables, and moderate amounts of protein. Desserts are light but sensuous; menus are varied and always tasty.

COLD SOUP OF WATERCRESS

1/2 onion, chopped
1 cup chicken stock
2 bunches watercress, stemmed and coarsely chopped
1 cup plain yogurt
Juice of 1 lemon
Freshly ground black pepper to taste
Vegetable salt to taste

Stir onion with chicken stock in a saucepan and bring to a boil. Add watercress, remove from heat, and cool mixture fast over ice. Stir in yogurt and lemon juice and season to taste. Serve ice cold.

SERVINGS: 1. CALORIES PER SERVING: 45

RED SNAPPER WITH CUCUMBER

2 pounds seedless cucumbers, unpeeled and sliced
Pinch salt
4 to 5 ounces raw, very fresh red snapper fillet, thinly
    sliced
1 tablespoon olive oil
1/4 cup peppercorns
Garnish: 2 lemon wedges

Sprinkle cucumbers with salt and set aside for about 15 minutes. Drain off any water, then arrange cucumber slices on individual serving plates. Arrange red snapper slices to cover cucumbers. Sprinkle with olive oil and peppercorns to taste. Serve cold with lemon wedges.

SERVINGS: 2. CALORIES PER SERVING: 150

TOMATOES STUFFED WITH COTTAGE CHEESE AND EGG

4 large fresh, ripe tomatoes
1 clove garlic, finely chopped
2 tablespoons cottage cheese
2 tablespoons tomato paste
1 tablespoon freshly grated Parmesan cheese
4 eggs

Preheat oven to 350 degrees.

Wash tomatoes and cut off tops. Scoop out insides and discard. Sprinkle insides of tomatoes lightly with salt and the garlic. Turn upside down to drain for about 30 minutes.

Mix cottage cheese with tomato paste and Parmesan. Place tomato shells in a nonstick pan. Carefully break an egg into each one and cover with cottage cheese mixture. Bake for 20 to 25 minutes.

Serve immediately.

SERVINGS: 4. CALORIES PER SERVING: 140

CARROT MOUSSE CAKE

1 1/2 pounds carrots, peeled and sliced
2 eggs plus 1 egg yolk, beaten
Salt and freshly ground black pepper to taste
Garnish: Sliced scallions

Preheat oven to 400 degrees. Cook carrots in boiling salted water till tender, then drain well and purée in blender. Mix purée well with eggs and egg yolk and season to taste. Pour mixture into 6 buttered ramekins and set in baking pan filled halfway with hot water. Bake for 35 minutes. When mousse is done, unmold each onto a serving plate and garnish with scallions. Serve immediately.

SERVINGS: 4. CALORIES PER SERVING: 120

CRABMEAT WITH COTTAGE CHEESE

8 ounces lumpy crabmeat
8 ounces cottage cheese
1 medium-size onion, finely chopped
1/8 teaspoon freshly grated nutmeg

Preheat oven to 400 degrees.

Mix crabmeat and cottage cheese well. Add chopped onion and nutmeg and season to taste. Spoon mixture into buttered dish and bake for 20 minutes. Serve immediately.

SERVINGS: 2. CALORIES PER SERVING: 220

CLAMS AND CAULIFLOWER SALAD

1 head cauliflower, trimmed
24 clams, shelled
2 teaspoons mixed salad herbs
1 clove garlic, finely chopped
1/4 cup mustard vinaigrette

Break cauliflower into florets; cook in a saucepan of boiling water till tender but still crisp. Let cool. Mix clams with cauliflower. Sprinkle with herbs and chopped garlic. Pour dressing on top, toss, and chill. Serve very cold.

SERVINGS: 4. CALORIES PER SERVINGS: 250

CUCUMBER STUFFED WITH SHRIMP

1 large cucumber
1 red bell pepper, seeded and chopped
Finely chopped fresh mint leaves, to taste
8 ounces shrimp, peeled, deveined, and rinsed
1/2 cup plain low-fat yogurt

Trim ends from cucumber, then slice crosswise into approximately 6 equal sections. Scoop out center of each section, leaving about 1/2-inch thickness all around. Mix together red pepper, mint, shrimp, and yogurt. Season to taste. Fill each cucumber section with mixture. Serve chilled.
SERVINGS: 2. CALORIES PER SERVING: 150

FOUR SEASONS SPA CHICKEN

1 large chicken breast, skinned, boned, and halved
Freshly ground black pepper
Pinch garlic powder
2 teaspoons finely chopped fresh basil
Garnish: Thin lime slices and chopped fresh herbs

Prepare charcoal fire in grill or preheat broiler.
Season chicken with pepper to taste and garlic powder. Press basil into chicken. Grill or broil chicken for about 4 minutes per side.
Slice chicken breast into long, thin slices along the grain. Arrange on a warm plate, garnished with paper-thin slices of lime and sprinkle with fresh herbs. Serve with steamed vegetables.
SERVINGS: 2. CALORIES PER SERVING: 195
Note: Chicken can also be cooked without fat in a nonstick skillet.

SKEWER OF MONKFISH, SOLE, AND SALMON WITH ORANGES

8 ounces each monkfish, sole, and salmon fillets
2 oranges, peeled and sectioned
Freshly ground black pepper to taste
2 tablespoons dry white wine

Prepare charcoal fire in grill or preheat broiler. Cut fish fillets
into 1 1/2-inch pieces. Alternating types of fish, skewer fish
cubes with a slice of orange in between each piece.

Broil or grill skewers for approximately 15 minutes. Season to taste. Sprinkle with white wine before serving on a
heated plate.

SERVINGS: 4. CALORIES PER SERVING: 325

STRAWBERRY MOUSSE

1 pint fresh strawberries
Low-calorie sweetener or confectioners' sugar to taste
  (optional)
4 egg whites, at room temperature
1/3 cup heavy cream, chilled
Garnish: Mint sprigs, strawberry slices, or candied violets

Hull berries. Purée in blender, then press through a fine
sieve to strain out seeds. Taste for sweetness; add sweetener
or sugar if necessary. Beat egg whites in large bowl till stiff
but not dry. Set aside. In small, well-chilled bowl, using
chilled beaters, beat cream till doubled in volume. Fold
whipped cream into purée, then fold purée and cream mixture into beaten egg whites. Spoon mousse into 4 tall dessert
glasses. Garnish and serve.

SERVINGS: 4. CALORIES PER SERVING: 145

APPLE COMPOTE

2 pounds tart apples
Juice of 1 lemon
2 tablespoons honey

Peel and core apples; place in a bowl. Blend lemon juice and honey and toss with apples to coat well. Serve chilled.
     CALORIES PER APPLE: 132

BAKED BANANAS

4 bananas, peeled
Juice of 1/2 lemon
1/4 cup honey
1/2 apple, peeled, cored, and grated

Preheat oven to 400 degrees.
     Slice each banana lengthwise in half and place halves cut side down on a long sheet of aluminum foil. Combine lemon juice and honey and drizzle over banana. Cover with grated apple. Close foil and bake for 10 minutes.
     Serve immediately.
     SERVINGS: 4. CALORIES PER SERVING: 200

POACHED APPLE SLICES

2 apples, peeled, cored, and cut into 1/2-inch slices
Juice of 1 lemon
1/4 cup honey
Ground cinnamon to taste

Poach apple slices, covered, in a little water till tender. Drain
well. Sprinkle apples with lemon juice, honey, and cinnamon. Serve cold.

SERVINGS: 4. CALORIES PER SERVING: 115

La Costa Hotel and Resort

Pacific breezes warm the winter air to an average of 68 degrees and supply naturally cool air averaging 74 degrees in summer. Lush green valleys and lofty mountains add to the atmosphere of serenity. In just such a setting the La Costa Hotel and Resort in Carlsbad, California, provides the ultimate in luxurious accommodations. The hotel is well known for its spa program, but that program is only one of the many reasons why people choose La Costa. In fact, most visitors are vacationers, not on the Spa Plan.

The resort is large (6,700 acres) and claims to have the most extensive facilities in the United States. Guests come to La Costa for the great golf and tennis, the fine food and entertainment, and a chance to relax on nearby beaches or beside one of the three pools (perhaps in the company of celebrities). They come to enjoy the many area attractions. San Diego is just thirty-five minutes away with its famous zoo, Sea World, Wild Animal Park, and the esteemed Shakespearean Old Globe Theater. To the north, (about a two-hour drive) are Disneyland, Knott's Berry Farm, and Hollywood; to the south (an hour away), Mexico.

The hotel has five excellent restaurants serving seafood, Continental, and elegant European cuisine. After dinner guests can listen to music, dance, or retire to the game room for bridge or backgammon. Current movies are shown nightly in the 202-seat La Costa Theater; HBO is available in all guest rooms.

The Davis Cup and the Clairol Crown are only two of the major tennis events which have been held on La Costa's twenty-five courts. Pancho Segura, trainer of Jimmy Connors, or one of the other five teaching pros are on hand for lessons. A tennis hostess matches partnerless guests with similarly skilled players. Golf director Tommy Jacobs, former PGA tour star, heads the staff at the La Costa twenty-seven-hole championship golf course, site of the annual MONY Tournament of Champions.

Accommodations vary from rooms and suites in the main building to chateaus, cottages, villas, and very private, exclusive executive homes. All guests, regardless of accommodations, receive a gift basket of La Costa health and beauty products and thick terrycloth La Costa robes to use during their stay. A gift shop and a "sportique" selling everything from jogging shoes to designer fashions are also on the premises.

Guests on the Spa Plan enjoy all of the above amenities and the special pampering services that combine to make up the "La Costa Look." The Spa Plan gives guests the opportunity to achieve greater inner and outer beauty through its diet and exercise program, its skin care and makeup products, and the La Costa Thirty-Day Regimen vitamin and mineral supplements. The Spa Plan includes three meals per day, all spa services, and tennis court time and greens fees.

The fitness regimens are more structured than the original spa plan, while retaining all of that plan's services, treatments, and other features. It also offers body composition testing—a state of the art computerized analysis of the body's fat content, water content, and lean muscle mass.

With their room confirmations, prospective spa guests receive a form to record food intake for one day. This form is returned to La Costa before arrival where it is put through a computer programmed to analyze dietary deficiencies and excesses. The computer analysis helps the spa's medical staff, headed by Dr. A. Gordon Reynolds, formulate an individualized, lifelong diet plan. After check-in spa guests are seen by Dr. Reynolds or one of his staff to determine their fitness level; they then confer with a spa counselor and dietician to work out a personal diet and exercise program.

Once their appropriate activity levels are determined, guests tone up and slim down in a variety of exercise classes that include a morning walk, yoga, dance, stretch and flex, spot reducing, "aquathinice" (pool exercises), rigorous calisthenics, and water volleyball (a highly spirited game for men only).

After exercise guests can enjoy a sauna, a private whirlpool bath, a rock steam room, and roman pool—or pamper themselves in a variety of sybaritic treatments.

Several kinds of facials (for women and men) are available at La Costa. Deep-pore cleaning is accomplished with a fine mist and Frimator brush. Pores are vacuumed and impurities whisked away. A pulsating massage follows to firm and smooth the skin, and then a special moisturizing masque. Collagen facials and high frequency treatment can also be requested.

The loofa treatment washes away scaly dried-out layers of skin all over the body. A rubdown with salts and fine oils is followed by a wrap in hot sheets saturated in herbs and spices. After a rest period, the body is gently massaged with loofa mitts and a fine warm-water spray. The final touch is a Swiss Shower—seventeen jets of water, their temperature and pressure constantly changing to produce an exhilarating tingle.

The Orthion System combines mechanical treatments with the use of traction to soothe, relax, and stimulate the entire nervous system. Orthion therapy is designed to relieve and prevent tension-oriented aches, pains, and spasms in the lower back, shoulders, legs, arms, and neck.

Ion baths provide relaxing circulatory treatments. Ionized steam, ozone, and oxygen open pores and activate respiration, resulting in fresher, more elastic skin. The ion bath is also considered an important aid in the treatment of cellulite.

The Sunbrella, a medically approved sun-tanning apparatus, is an effective way to accelerate tanning with little danger of burning. Supervised and used in short periods, the Sunbrella allows guests to tan front and back without turning over.

La Costa's Spa Plan meals are sugar and salt free, but retain the epicurean quality of the food served in all the resort's restaurants. Chef Willy Hauser, whose thirty-six years of culinary experience includes posts at several fine European and American resorts, has created recipes that keep calories to a minimum—but not at the expense of taste.

All meals begin with low-calorie salads and soups.

SPA FRENCH DRESSING

2 rounded teaspoons vegetable gum (see note below)
1/2 cup distilled white vinegar
1 1/2 cups unsweetened pineapple juice
Juice of 1/2 lemon
1/4 teaspoon dry mustard
1/8 teaspoon freshly ground white pepper
3 heaping teaspoons paprika
Pinch ground celery seed

Dissolve vegetable gum in a small amount of the vinegar. Mix remaining vinegar with pineapple juice, lemon juice, mustard, pepper, paprika, and celery seed in small bowl. Blend lightly with a wire whip or fork; do not overbeat. (If the dressing is overbeaten, the air incorporated will dilute the color.) Place in a covered container and store in refrigerator till needed.

MAKES ABOUT 2 1/4 CUPS. CALORIES PER TABLESPOON: 10

Note: There are many kinds of vegetable gum and it can be purchased from your pharmacist.

LA COSTA SPA VINAIGRETTE DRESSING

1/4 cup distilled white vinegar
1 cup unsweetened pineapple juice
Juice of 1/2 lemon
1/4 teaspoon dry mustard
1 clove garlic, crushed
Coarsely ground black pepper to taste
1/4 cup finely chopped celery hearts
1/4 cup finely chopped fresh chives or scallion tops
1/4 cup finely chopped mixed green and red bell peppers

Combine all ingredients except chopped vegetables in small bowl. Beat lightly or strain to remove all lumps. Add chopped vegetables, place in a covered container, and refrigerate till needed.

MAKES ABOUT 2 CUPS. CALORIES PER TABLESPOON: 10

Note: Chopped fresh vegetables may be added just before serving.

LA COSTA SPA ICED GAZPACHO

1 small zucchini, cut up
2 tablespoons chopped fresh chives
1/2 green bell pepper, seeded and diced
1 cucumber, diced
2 small tomatoes, peeled, seeded, and diced
1/2 jalapeño pepper, seeded and diced
1/2 clove garlic, minced
1 cup salt-free tomato juice
1/2 cup beef bouillon

Place all ingredients in a blender and blend for a few seconds, or till vegetables are finely chopped. Chill well. Serve in chilled soup cups.

SERVINGS: 4. CALORIES PER SERVING: 25

LA COSTA SPA TOMATO SOUP

2 1/2 cups unsalted, defatted chicken broth
3/4 cup low-sodium tomato purée
1/2 medium-size fresh, ripe tomato, chopped
1/2 small carrot, chopped
1 celery stalk, chopped
4 fresh parsley sprigs
1 bay leaf
Pinch dried oregano
Pinch dried basil
Small pinch garlic powder
Small pinch freshly ground white pepper
Small pinch dried dillweed

Combine all ingredients in a saucepan and simmer, uncovered, for 30 minutes. Strain. Serve hot in bouillon cups.

SERVINGS: 4. CALORIES PER SERVING: 40

LA COSTA SPA PURÉE OF VEGETABLE SOUP

2 cups unsalted, defatted chicken broth
2 medium-size carrots, peeled and chopped
1/2 cup chopped rutabaga
3/4 cup chopped turnip
1 tablespoon chopped onion
Small pinch freshly ground white pepper
Pinch ground celery seed
1/2 cup skim milk

Bring chicken broth to a boil in a saucepan and add carrot, rutabaga, turnip, onion, and seasonings. Bring the liquid back to a boil and cook, uncovered, till vegetables are tender. Cool slightly and purée in a blender. Return to saucepan, reheat, and stir in milk. Serve hot in bouillon cups.
    SERVINGS: 4. CALORIES PER SERVING: 50

All diet meals are served in a separate dining room or may be ordered through room service. Regular meals for dieters, guests, or companions not on the Spa Plan can also be ordered. Entrées consist of 150- to 200-calorie dishes, and even desserts are low-cal—about 40 calories per serving.

LA COSTA SPA RAGOUT OF VEAL

12 ounces trimmed boneless veal, cut into 1-inch cubes
1 large onion, chopped
1/2 cup dry red wine
1 can (16 ounces) salt-free whole tomatoes
1 can (6 ounces) tomato purée
1 teaspoon paprika
Freshly ground black pepper to taste
Garnish: Julienne of carrot, rutabaga, and turnip

Brown meat over high heat in a large nonstick skillet. Reduce heat; add onion and wine. Stir to scrape browned bits from bottom of skillet. Add tomatoes, tomato purée, paprika, and pepper. Cover and simmer about 45 to 60 minutes, or till meat is tender. Garnish with julienne of vegetables to serve.

SERVINGS: 4. CALORIES PER SERVING: 146

LA COSTA SPA CHICKEN CACCIATORE

2 shallots, chopped
1/2 small green bell pepper, seeded and chopped
1/2 cup sliced fresh mushrooms
1/2 cup dry white wine
1 can (8 ounces) salt-free whole tomatoes
1/8 teaspoon garlic powder
4 chicken pieces (3 ounces each), poached (allow 20
    percent weight for bone)
Scant teaspoon each of freshly ground black pepper, dried
    rosemary, dried oregano, dried basil, and fennel
    seeds
Artificial sweetener (optional)

Simmer shallots, green pepper, and mushrooms in wine, uncovered, in medium-size skillet till tender. Add tomatoes, bring to a boil, then allow to simmer, uncovered, till reduced by one half in volume, about 15 to 30 minutes. Stir occasionally. Add garlic powder, pepper, herbs, and fennel seeds and simmer, covered, an additional 30 minutes. Add artificial sweetener to taste if tomatoes are bitter.

Pour 1 tablespoon of sauce over each piece of chicken and serve.

SERVINGS: 4. CALORIES PER SERVING: 146

LA COSTA SPA BOUILLABAISSE

Pinch saffron threads
1/2 cup dry white wine
4 clams, shelled
1 celery stalk, trimmed and chopped
1 small onion, chopped
8 cups water
1 clove garlic, smashed
1 leek (white part with one inch of green), thinly
    sliced
1/2 teaspoon fennel seeds
1 large fresh, ripe tomato, peeled, seeded, and diced
Freshly ground black pepper to taste
1 rock lobster tail, quartered
4 ounces red snapper, quartered
4 ounces shrimp, shelled, deveined, and rinsed
4 ounces scallops

Soak saffron threads in white wine; set aside.

To make clam stock, simmer clams, celery, and onion, uncovered, in water in a saucepan for 10 minutes. Strain stock and reserve clams.

In a large nonstick saucepan, heat garlic clove slightly but do not brown; discard. Add sliced leek, fennel seeds, and saffron/wine mixture to saucepan; simmer, uncovered, for 3 minutes. Add diced tomato and simmer 5 minutes longer.

Add clam stock and pepper; bring to a boil. Add lobster tail, red snapper, shrimp, and scallops to stock. Lower heat and simmer for 10 minutes. Add clams to heat through, and serve.

SERVINGS: 4. CALORIES PER SERVING: 200

LA COSTA SPA BAKED LASAGNE

1 small onion, chopped
2 cloves garlic, minced
1/4 cup dry white wine
8 ounces fresh mushrooms, sliced
1 can (16 ounces) salt-free whole tomatoes, crushed
1 1/2 cups tomato purée
The following to taste: dried oregano, dried basil, freshly
    ground black pepper, bay leaf, dried rosemary,
    chopped fresh parsley, fennel seeds
2 ounces fresh spinach, chopped
1 egg, beaten
6 ounces dry-curd bakers' or cottage cheese
1/2 cup plus 2 tablespoons freshly grated Parmesan
    cheese
6 ounces lasagne noodles
2 ounces mozzarella cheese, thinly sliced

In a large saucepan, simmer onion and garlic in wine till soft
but not browned. Add sliced mushrooms and cook, uncovered, until liquid evaporates. Add crushed tomatoes with
juice, tomato purée, and seasonings to taste. Simmer sauce,
uncovered, for 45 minutes, stirring occasionally to prevent
sticking. Add chopped spinach at the last moment. Measure out and reserve 1 1/2 cups of sauce for serving with
lasagne.

Boil lasagne noodles according to package directions.
While noodles are boiling, combine bakers cheese, egg, and
the 1/2 cup Parmesan cheese. Drain noodles.

Preheat oven to 400 degrees. Spray bottom of a 7 ×
7-inch baking dish with low-fat vegetable coating. Begin with
a layer of one fourth of noodles. Cover with one fourth of
tomato sauce, and then one fourth of bakers' cheese mixture. Repeat 3 times. Cover last layer of cheese mixture
with thin slices of mozzarella cheese and the 2 tablespoons

Parmesan cheese. Place casserole in oven and bake for about 45 minutes, or till top is brown and sauce is bubbly.

Serve hot, with extra sauce and Parmesan cheese.

SERVINGS: 8. CALORIES PER SERVING: 200

LA COSTA SPA BAKED APPLES

6 small tart, firm apples
1/2 teaspoon low-calorie sweetener
1/2 teaspoon ground cinnamon
3/4 cup water
1/2 cup unsweetened apple juice
1 stick whole cinnamon
2 whole cloves

Preheat oven to 375 degrees.

Prepare apples for baking; wash, pare, and remove top quarter of peel. Place in a shallow heavy pan that has a tight lid. Pack apples in pan closely. Mix sweetener and ground cinnamon in the water; stir in apple juice. Pour liquid and whole spices around the apples. Cover and bake in oven till fork tender. Serve at once or, if apples are to be served cold, store, covered, in refrigerator.

SERVINGS: 6. CALORIES PER SERVING: 40

LA COSTA SPA FRUIT PARFAIT

2 cups frozen unsweetened boysenberries, blueberries, or strawberries
1 1/2 teaspoons unflavored gelatin
Low-calorie sweetener to taste
2 teaspoons lime juice

Sprinkle gelatin over just enough cold water to dissolve it.

Thaw berries, retaining the juice. Measure amount of juice obtained and add water if necessary to measure 1 1/2 cups total. Combine the boysenberry juice and gelatin. Allow to set for 20 minutes. Combine the berries, thickened juice, sweetener, and lime juice. Refrigerate till slightly thickened, then spoon into 4 parfait glasses and chill till ready to serve.

SERVINGS: 4. CALORIES PER SERVING: 40

LA COSTA SPA COUPE SAINT-JACQUES

1 teaspoon unflavored gelatin
1 1/2 cups very fresh buttermilk
1 cup skim milk
2 tablespoons vanilla extract
1 teaspoon grated lemon zest
1 cup canned unsweetened, pitted cherries
Low-calorie sweetener to taste
Garnish: 1/2 cup chopped watermelon, 1/2 cup chopped
        cantaloupe, 1/2 cup chopped honeydew melon

Soften gelatin in a few drops of water until completely dissolved and combine with buttermilk, milk, and vanilla in a blender. Beat mixture till frothy. Add lemon zest, cherries, and sweetener and blend again for 15 seconds.

Place mixture in a shallow pan in the freezer and freeze until a "mushy" consistency is attained. Beat the sherbet again, with a wire whisk or fork, to incorporate air and keep the ice crystals small; repeat every 15 to 20 minutes till sherbet is frozen.

Remove sherbet to the refrigerator 30 minutes before serving. Garnish each serving with 1 tablespoon each of the chopped fruit. Serve immediately.

SERVINGS: 8. CALORIES PER SERVING: 40

The Greenhouse

A complete spa in a solarium and the only year-round health resort for women under a single roof, The Greenhouse in Arlington, Texas (midway between Dallas and Fort Worth), offers its guests both privacy and pampering. The portico entrance to the spa is unmarked, most of the guest rooms have no outside doors, and there is round-the-clock security. Under the latticed glass roof, lush gardens and patios surround the luxurious spa building, which contains pool and gymnasium, drawing room and dining room. A staff of 125 specialists sees to each guest's every need.

Executive director Toni Beck has been associated with the spa since its founding in 1965, while also acting as chairman of the dance department at Southern Methodist University, playing an active role in the Dallas arts community, and authoring two books, *Fashion Your Figure* and *Focus Your Figure*. Beck is listed in both *Who's Who in America* and *Who's Who of American Women*. A dancer, Beck believes that getting in touch with one's body physically is the beginning of mental and emotional self-knowledge. The exercise program she has developed for The Greenhouse employs minimal equipment (barbells, exercycles, resistance machines, etc.) and is based on a modified dancer's regimen—maximum control in a graceful, efficient series of movements and countermovements.

Beck abhors exercise programs that seek to make beanpoles out of every woman. "I say this is what I think can happen with your body with the proper exercises. If you hate exercise per se, try and find some physical things you like to do, such as walking, dancing, bicycle riding, swimming."

The Greenhouse's fitness program emphasizes two principles: (1) like your body—it's the only one you've got; (2) use your body effectively in exercise, developing consistency and motivation.

"No one has a perfect body," Beck says. "I've worked on this one for thirty-seven years. Everyone has to work. No one gets a free ride."

Elizabeth Taylor, Ann Landers, and Brooke Shields have all consulted Beck, as has the Duchess of Windsor.

"Cellulite and flab are great levelers," Beck once told a reporter. "It happens to housewives, but believe me it happens to royalty, too."

At The Greenhouse, guests exercise four and a half hours a day. Each woman's personal schedule is supervised and guided by a staff of skilled technicians. Physical activity is interspersed with soothing massage, sauna, and whirlpool comforts. A comprehensive beauty program has been designed by Charles of the Ritz and incorporates skin care products from the exclusive French line of Rene Guinot.

Guests can enjoy all the spa's amenities without going outside, although there are outdoor jogging paths, an outdoor pool, and tennis courts on the grounds. Tennis lessons can be scheduled or guests may take advantage of the spa's weekly limousine service to Nieman-Marcus in downtown Dallas.

Like the exercise program, the diet plan at The Greenhouse has been a proven success for many years. Based on sound, nonfaddish nutrition, the recipes developed by the late Helen Corbitt have remained consistently popular with dieters and nondieters alike.

A variety of dressings perk up green salads, vegetables, and seafoods.

NO-CALORIE DRESSING

1/2 cup wine vinegar
1/2 teaspoon vegetable salt
1/2 clove garlic, crushed
1 tablespoon chopped fresh parsley
Pinch dried oregano, dried tarragon, or curry powder

Mix ingredients together well.
MAKES ABOUT 1/2 CUP. CALORIES PER TABLESPOON: 2

GREEN HERB DRESSING

1/4 cup chopped fresh parsley
1/4 cup watercress leaves
4 scallions, chopped
1 teaspoon dry mustard
1/4 cup water
1 egg yolk
1/4 cup safflower oil
1/4 cup tarragon vinegar
1/2 teaspoon mixed salad herbs
1/2 teaspoon prepared horseradish

Mix all ingredients in blender or by hand with a whisk.
MAKES ABOUT 1 1/2 CUPS. CALORIES PER TABLESPOON: 32
Note: A favorite for both seafood and green salads, some guests order it at every meal.

VINAIGRETTE DRESSING

1 tablespoon Dijon mustard
2 tablespoons lemon juice
2 tablespoons vinegar
6 tablespoons safflower oil
Vegetable salt to taste
1/2 teaspoon freshly ground black pepper
6 tablespoons water

Put all ingredients but the water in a bowl and beat for 1 minute with a whisk. Beat in the water a little at a time.
MAKES ABOUT 1 CUP. CALORIES PER TABLESPOON: 48
Note: Great for marinating vegetables, seafood, and greens.
Variations: For Mimosa Dressing, add 1 hard-cooked egg white, finely diced or sieved, and 2 tablespoons finely chopped fresh parsley. For Niçoise Dressing, add 1/2 clove garlic, minced; 2 tablespoons minced onion; and 2 tablespoons chopped fresh parsley.

Low calorie soups are served before dinner or as a snack or "pick-me-up."

CLAM AND MUSHROOM SOUP

3 cups chicken broth
1/4 cup thinly sliced onion
1 cup minced clams
1/2 cup thinly sliced fresh or canned mushrooms
Few bean threads or cellophane noodles
2 tablespoons chopped fresh parsley
Vegetable salt to taste

Combine broth, onion, clams, and mushrooms in a saucepan and bring to a boil. Cover and boil 1 minute. Add bean threads and cook till transparent. Remove from heat, add parsley and vegetable salt, and serve.

SERVINGS: 6. CALORIES PER SERVING: 41

Note: Bean threads may be purchased at better food markets or Oriental food shops.

MINTED PEA SOUP

1 teaspoon whipped margarine
1/4 cup finely diced onion
1 1/2 cups chicken broth
1 1/2 cups frozen peas
2 iceberg or romaine lettuce leaves
1/4 cup chopped fresh parsley
Few leaves of fresh mint
1 cup skim milk
Garnish: Chopped chives or grated orange peel

Melt margarine in a saucepan. Add onion and 1/2 cup of the chicken broth. Cook over medium heat till onion is soft. Add peas, lettuce, parsley, and mint. Cover and boil for 2 minutes. Add remaining broth and bring to a boil. Remove from heat and let cool.

Put cooled soup in a blender or food processor and blend till smooth. Stir in milk, then chill.

Garnish and serve.

SERVINGS: 6. CALORIES PER SERVING: 25

Note: Also good hot.

Diets for weight loss are based on 850 calories a day; meals are supplemented with midmorning broth and an afternoon fruit frappe. About 10 percent of The Greenhouse's guests don't wish to lose weight, so rolls, muffins, and desserts are available to add calories where desired.

All meals are enhanced by beautiful appointments of china, linen, and silver. An elegant breakfast tray is delivered to each guest's room along with her personal schedule for the day. Luncheon is poolside; dinner is more formal and guests dress appropriately. It is the only time they are seen in clothes other than swim suits or the spa-provided navy leotards and tights or yellow terry robes. A light appetizer is served by the pool before dinner; Wednesday evening is designated as an evening of rest and dinner is served in the guests' rooms.

Corbitt's recipes are colorful and innovative, using a variety of foods to appeal to many palates. Protein dishes containing eggs, cheese, seafood, and poultry make up many of the entrées served at The Greenhouse.

ORIENTAL BEEF

5 ounces lean beef, thinly sliced
1 tablespoon dry sherry
2 tablespoons soy sauce (see note below)
1 teaspoon vegetable oil
1/2 clove garlic, crushed
1/4 cup thinly sliced onion
1/4 cup thinly sliced celery
3 fresh mushrooms, thinly sliced
1/4 cup thinly sliced green bell pepper
1/4 medium-size fresh, ripe tomato, peeled and sliced
   lengthwise

Pour sherry and soy sauce over meat and marinate for about 30 minutes. Heat oil, with garlic, in a skillet over medium high heat. Add onion and marinated beef; stir rapidly for 30 seconds. Add remaining ingredients, cover, and cook 2 minutes. Serve at once.

SERVINGS: 1. CALORIES PER SERVING: 195

Note: If you do not like the flavor of soy, omit it and use 3 tablespoons sherry.

SPANISH EGGS

1 teaspoon whipped margarine
1/2 cup sliced onion
1 clove garlic, crushed
1/2 cup chopped celery
1/4 cup sliced green bell pepper
2 cups peeled, seeded, and chopped tomatoes
1 bay leaf
4 whole cloves
1 teaspoon vegetable salt
6 eggs
Garnish: 1/4 cup chopped fresh parsley

Melt margarine in a saucepan. Add onion, garlic, celery, and green pepper. Sauté till soft, but do not brown. Add tomatoes, bay leaf, and cloves. Cook, uncovered, till thickened. Add vegetable salt.

Heat 3 to 4 inches of water in a saucepan. Bring to a boil. Stir simmering water to make a swirl. Slip egg into the middle of the swirl. Reduce heat to low. Cook egg for 3 to 5 minutes, then remove to a serving dish. Repeat procedure 5 times.

Remove bay leaf and cloves from sauce, and pour 1/4 cup over each of the poached eggs. Serve immediately.

SERVINGS: 6. CALORIES PER SERVING: 154

Note: This recipe makes 3 cups of sauce, enough for 12 eggs. Leftover sauce keeps well refrigerated or frozen.

GREEN CHILI TORTE

1 1/2 cups skim milk
2 eggs
1 1/4 cups shredded Monterey Jack cheese
1 can (4 ounces) whole green chilies, seeded and finely
    diced
1/4 teaspoon vegetable salt
Pinch red (cayenne) pepper

Preheat oven to 325 degrees.
    Heat milk in a small saucepan till hot but not boiling. Beat
eggs; slowly beat milk into them. Add cheese, chilies, and
seasonings. Pour into 6 lightly greased shirred-egg dishes or
one 9-inch pie pan. Bake for about 40 minutes, or till set.
    SERVINGS: 6. CALORIES PER SERVING: 111

STUFFED FLOUNDER

4 ounces shrimp, cooked and chopped
1 egg, lightly beaten
1/2 cup skim milk
1 tablespoon whipped margarine
1/2 cup chopped fresh mushrooms
1 teaspoon chopped fresh chives
1 teaspoon all-purpose flour
1 whole flounder (about 1 pound) cleaned and boned but
    head and tail left on)
2 teaspoons dry sherry
Vegetable salt to taste
Paprika to taste

Preheat oven to 350 degrees.
    Combine shrimp, egg, and 1/4 cup of the milk; set aside.

Melt margarine in small skillet. Sauté mushrooms and chives 1 minute. Add flour and cook, stirring, till bubbly. Add shrimp mixture and cook till thickened.

Split flounder, separating top from bottom. Place bottom half, skin side down, in a lightly greased shallow baking dish. Spread shrimp mixture over fish in baking dish and top with other flounder half, skin side up. Combine remaining 1/4 cup milk and sherry and pour over fish; sprinkle with seasonings. Bake for 30 minutes, or till fish flakes.

SERVINGS: 4. CALORIES PER SERVING: 304

SHRIMP CREOLE

1 tablespoon whipped margarine
1/2 cup sliced onion
1 clove garlic, crushed
1/2 cup sliced celery
1/4 cup sliced green bell pepper
2 cups peeled, seeded, and chopped tomatoes
1 bay leaf
4 whole cloves
24 medium shrimp, shelled, deveined, and rinsed
1 teaspoon vegetable salt
1 cup okra, trimmed and steamed 4 minutes
Garnish: 1/4 cup chopped fresh parsley

Melt margarine in a saucepan. Sauté onion, garlic, celery, and green pepper till soft, but do not brown. Add tomatoes, bay leaf, and cloves. Cook, uncovered, till thickened. Uncover and add shrimp; cover again and cook 3 minutes. Remove from heat. Season with vegetable salt, then remove bay leaf and cloves.

Serve over okra and sprinkle with chopped parsley.

SERVINGS: 4. CALORIES PER SERVING: 100

COQ AU VIN

1 tablespoon chopped shallots
2 Rock Cornish hens, cut up
4 whole small white onions
3/4 cup beef consommé
3/4 cup dry red wine
16 whole small fresh mushrooms
Vegetable salt to taste
Freshly ground black pepper to taste
Garnish: 2 tablespoons chopped fresh parsley

Heat broiler.

Spray ovenproof skillet with low-fat vegetable coating or brush with small amount of vegetable oil. Heat skillet. Add shallots and sauté for 1 minute. Add hens, skin side up, then place skillet under broiler till hens are browned. Add onions, consommé, and red wine. Cover and let simmer on top of stove for 30 minutes.

Add mushrooms to skillet and cook, uncovered, over high heat till liquid is reduced to one quarter of its original volume. Season, sprinkle with parsley, and serve.

SERVINGS: 4. CALORIES PER SERVING: 137

Because vegetables, as a rule, contain fewer calories and more vitamins and minerals than other foods they appear often on Greenhouse tables—steamed or stir-fried to minimize loss of valuable nutritional elements.

STIR-FRIED VEGETABLES

1 tablespoon peanut or vegetable oil
1/2 cup slivered carrots
1/2 cup slivered celery
1 medium-size zucchini, thinly sliced diagonally

2 tablespoons chicken broth or water
4 ounces snow peas
Vegetable salt to taste
Optional garnish: Chopped fresh parsley

Heat oil in a skillet over high heat till very hot. Add carrots
and stir-fry for 1 minute. Add celery and zucchini and stir
1 minute. Add chicken broth; cover and cook 30 seconds.
Add snow peas; cover and cook 30 seconds more (see note
below). Season with vegetable salt and soy sauce, if
desired. Stir and serve at once, with or without chopped
parsley.

SERVINGS: 6. CALORIES PER SERVING: 34

Note: If peas are large, add with celery and zucchini.
Variation: Any vegetable combination may be used.

ZUCCHINI CUPS

2 medium-large zucchini, ends trimmed off, cut into thirds
    crosswise
1 tablespoon whipped margarine
1 cup finely diced fresh mushrooms
1 tablespoon minced shallots or scallions
Vegetable salt to taste
1 tablespoon chopped fresh parsley
1 tablespoon freshly grated Parmesan cheese

Preheat oven to 350 degrees.

Steam zucchini pieces for 5 minutes. Cool and stand each
piece on end. Dig out center seeds, leaving a thin layer in the
bottom. Set aside.

Melt margarine in a skillet. Add mushrooms and shallots
and sauté for 2 minutes. Add vegetable salt and parsley. Fill
cavities of squash with mixture. Sprinkle with cheese. Place
in baking pan and bake till zucchini is reheated.

SERVINGS: 6. CALORIES PER SERVING: 34

TARRAGON TOMATOES

3 fresh, ripe tomatoes
1 clove garlic, minced
1/8 teaspoon dried tarragon
1/8 teaspoon freshly cracked black pepper
Few sprinklings of Parmesan cheese

Preheat oven to 350 degrees.
    Cut tomatoes in half. Combine garlic, tarragon, pepper, and cheese. Sprinkle over tomatoes; place in baking dish and bake till tender, about 30 minutes.
    SERVINGS: 6. CALORIES PER SERVING: 19

Not all guests of The Greenhouse need low-calorie regimes. About 10 percent are on maintenance diets, and a few actually come to the spa to gain weight. Everyone, dieting or not, enjoys The Greenhouse's famous cheesecake and other dessert delights.

LOW-CALORIE CHEESECAKE

1 envelope unflavored gelatin
2 tablespoons lemon juice
1/2 cup skim milk, scalded
2 eggs, separated
2 teaspoons low-calorie sweetener
2 1/2 cups low-fat ricotta cheese
1 cup crushed ice
1 teaspoon grated orange zest

Dissolve gelatin in lemon juice; add hot milk. Put in blender with egg yolks, sweetener, and cheese. Process at high speed for 2 minutes. Add crushed ice. Continue running at high speed till mixture is thoroughly blended. Beat egg whites till stiff. Fold into cheese mixture, along with orange zest. Pour into an 8-inch spring-form pan. Chill till firm, about 24 hours. Serve with any kind of puréed fresh fruit.

SERVINGS: 8. CALORIES PER SERVING: 67

COLD LEMON SOUFFLÉ

1 envelope unflavored gelatin
1/4 cup cold water
2 cups skim milk
4 egg yolks, beaten
Low-calorie sweetener to taste
1/2 cup lemon juice
2 tablespoons grated lemon zest
8 egg whites, stiffly beaten

Dissolve gelatin in cold water. Bring milk to a boil. Remove from heat and pour a little of the milk slowly into egg yolks in bowl, beating constantly. Add mixture to milk in saucepan. Cook till thick. Add gelatin; remove from heat and let cool.

Add sweetener, lemon juice, and lemon zest to cooled mixture. As mixture begins to congeal, fold in egg whites. Pour into a 2-quart soufflé dish and refrigerate.

Serve chilled.

SERVINGS: 4. CALORIES PER SERVING: 76

Variations: Use orange juice and orange zest, or lime juice and lime zest, instead of lemon.

HOT APRICOT WHIP

1 cup dried apricots
2 slices lemon
1 teaspoon low-calorie sweetener
4 egg whites, stiffly beaten

Place apricots in a saucepan and cover with water. Add lemon and simmer till apricots are soft and water is absorbed. Purée lemon and apricots in blender or food processor till smooth. Add sweetener. Cool.

Preheat oven to 350 degrees.

Stir one third of beaten egg whites into apricot mixture; fold in the rest. Pour into a lightly greased 1 1/2-quart casserole. Bake for 30 minutes, while you are eating your entrée.

Serve immediately.

SERVINGS: 6. CALORIES PER SERVING: 81

Demitasse after dinner is followed by selected entertainment and informal socializing.

Younger women, better informed about fitness and more subject to stress than previous generations, make up a large part of The Greenhouse's clientele. In this temperature-controlled atmosphere, women (a maximum of thirty-eight per week) can relax, freed from everyday cares and decision making, and begin to attain a heightened sense of self-awareness. More than 75 percent of The Greenhouse's guests come back, formidable proof of the spa's effectiveness.

Sans Souci

Sans Souci (French for "without care") is a coed weight control and fitness resort located fifteen miles southeast of Dayton, Ohio. And peace of mind is precisely what registered nurse Susanne Kircher, owner and director of the resort, tries to give her guests. With a staff of ten and a guest list limited to six at a time, the resort is able to provide personalized attention to each visitor.

The emphasis at Sans Souci is on behavior modification —freeing guests from addiction to food and providing strength of both body and mind to achieve serenity. Kircher, a native of Romania, acted as a nutrition consultant to Olympic teams in Europe for over fourteen years. She conducts most of the classes herself, although the staff includes licensed massage therapists and an exercise teacher with a degree in dance and psychology.

Set in a secluded wooded area adjoining the 600-acre Sugarcreek Reserve, the facilities include luxuriously appointed guest suites, an exercise room with Jacuzzi bath, a heated swimming pool, and an eighteen-station parcourse. Because most exercise classes are held outdoors, the resort's residential programs run from May through October. During winter sessions classes meet three times a week for two and a half hours and consist of exercise and education in nutrition, stress management, or other appropriate topics. A smoking cessation clinic is also presented. There is an additional charge for massages, facials, herbal wraps, and loofa scrubs.

With a physician's approval, guests interested in even greater weight loss than the average pound a day can fast for one day, taking only liquids at two- to three-hour intervals. Kircher and her staff have devised some interesting drinks for these guests.

ALMOND MILK

12 blanched whole almonds
3/4 cup water
3 ice cubes
Dash vanilla extract
1 small ripe banana
Garnish: Dash freshly grated nutmeg

Combine almonds, water, ice cubes, and vanilla in blender. Cover and blend till smooth. Add banana; cover and blend again till smooth. Pour into glasses, sprinkle nutmeg on top, and serve immediately.

SERVINGS: 2. CALORIES PER SERVING: 79

PROTEIN DRINK

1/2 cup skim milk
1 egg white
1/2 to 1 teaspoon brewed decaffeinated coffee
Low-calorie sweetener to taste
Ice cubes to fill blender

Blend all ingredients in blender till smooth.
> SERVINGS: 1. CALORIES PER SERVING: 60
> *Note:* Use less ice if thicker drink desired.

SANS SOUCI SHAKE

4 to 5 fresh or frozen strawberries
4 to 5 fresh or frozen melon balls (cantaloupe, honeydew,
   or watermelon)
1/4 ripe banana or 2 orange slices or 3 pineapple
   chunks
Ice cubes to fill blender
Low-calorie sweetener to taste

Blend all ingredients in blender till smooth.
> SERVINGS: 1. CALORIES PER SERVING: 80 TO 90
> *Note:* Use less ice if thicker drink desired.

PIÑA COLADA

3 heaping tablespoons instant nonfat dry milk
1 capful each of rum, coconut, and pineapple
   extract
1 cup water
Low-calorie sweetener to taste
Ice cubes to fill blender
Pineapple chunks (optional)
1 can (6 ounces) unsweetened pineapple juice

Blend all ingredients except juice till smooth. Pour 1/4 cup
juice in bottom of each of 3 glasses and pour blended mixture
over it for a layered effect.
> SERVINGS: 3. CALORIES PER SERVING (WITHOUT THE PINE-
> APPLE): 75
> *Note:* Use less ice if thicker drink desired.

Other liquid specialties at the resort include the soups—both hot and cold.

COLD CANTALOUPE SOUP

1 fresh cantaloupe, peeled, seeded, and sliced
2 to 3 tablespoons plain low-fat yogurt
Ice cubes to fill blender
Low-calorie sweetener to taste
Ground cinnamon to taste

Fill blender with cantaloupe slices, yogurt, and ice. Add sweetener and cinnamon. Blend till smooth.
  SERVINGS: 2. CALORIES PER SERVING: 55

COLD CUCUMBER SOUP

1 1/2 cups plain low-fat yogurt
1 small clove garlic, minced
1 tablespoon tarragon vinegar
1/2 teaspoon finely shredded lemon zest
1/2 teaspoon dried dillweed
Dash ground red (cayenne) pepper
1/4 cup water or chicken broth
1 small cucumber, peeled and shredded
2 tablespoons chopped fresh parsley
Optional garnish: Chopped fresh chives

In blender combine yogurt, garlic, tarragon vinegar, lemon zest, dillweed, and cayenne; blend well. Add water or chicken broth; blend till smooth. Pour yogurt mixture over cucumber in a mixing bowl; stir in parsley. Cover and chill 4 hours or overnight. Garnish with chopped chives, if desired.
  SERVINGS: 4. CALORIES PER SERVING: 53

ZUCCHINI SOUP

6 zucchini, sliced
1/4 cup butter buds
The following to taste: dried rosemary, garlic, ground red
    (cayenne) pepper, vegetable salt
1/4 cup chicken broth

Sauté zucchini in butter substitute in a saucepan until tender.
Sprinkle with seasonings, then blend in chicken broth. Reheat until boiling.
    SERVINGS: 4. CALORIES PER SERVING: 42

CASHEW CARROT SOUP

2 medium-size onions, chopped
2 cups shredded cabbage, greens, or chard
2 cups grated carrots
1 cup chopped apple
5 cups chicken stock
2 fresh, ripe tomatoes, peeled, seeded, and chopped, or 2
    tablespoons tomato paste
1/3 cup brown rice (soaked)
1/2 cup coarsely chopped cashews
1/2 cup raisins
Herb seasonings and vegetable salt to taste
Garnish: 1 cup plain low-fat yogurt

Combine all ingredients except seasonings and garnish in
soup kettle or large saucepan. Bring to a boil. Let simmer,
uncovered, for 8 minutes. Remove from heat and season.
Serve each portion topped with a dollop of yogurt.
    SERVINGS: 6. CALORIES PER SERVING: 48

LENTIL RICE SOUP

1 cup dried lentils
1 onion, chopped
1 bay leaf
2 whole cloves
1/4 cup chicken stock
1 carrot, chopped
1 celery stalk, chopped
1/2 teaspoon dried tarragon
Vegetable salt to taste
1/4 teaspoon freshly ground black pepper
8 cups water
1/2 cup brown rice

Place lentils in a saucepan and cover with water; soak for a few hours or overnight. Drain and add all ingredients except rice. Cook over low heat, covered, about 1 hour, or till lentils are soft. After 1 hour, add brown rice. Cook longer, stirring occasionally. Remove from heat. With a wooden spoon, crush some of the cooked lentils to thicken soup. Remove bay leaf and cloves before serving.

SERVINGS: 10. CALORIES PER SERVING: 56

Menus at the spa cater to guests' tastes and possible allergies. The vegetarian-based diet consists of 500 to 800 calories a day. Raw fruits and vegetables are served often; other foods are cooked as briefly as possible to avoid overcooking, which destroys vitamins and minerals. Fish and lean poultry appear two or three times a week in dishes like Chicken Paprikash or Seafood Divan.

CHICKEN PAPRIKASH

1/4 cup chopped onion
1/4 cup chopped green bell pepper
Vegetable oil
4 1/2 teaspoons Hungarian-style paprika
1/2 teaspoon dried marjoram
2 chicken breasts, split and skin removed
3/4 cup chicken broth
3 ounces ricotta cheese
1 teaspoon arrowroot
Vegetable salt to taste
Garnish: 2 tablespoons chopped fresh parsley

Preheat oven to 350 degrees.

Sauté onion and green pepper in small amount of heated oil in a heavy ovenproof skillet till tender but not brown. Sprinkle with 3 teaspoons of the paprika and the marjoram and stir to combine. Top with chicken breasts; sprinkle with remaining 1 1/2 teaspoons paprika. Cover and bake for 35 to 40 minutes, or till chicken is fork-tender.

Add chicken broth to skillet; simmer on range top 2 to 3 minutes. Remove chicken breasts; keep warm. Pour contents of skillet into blender; add cheese and arrowroot and blend till smooth.

Return chicken breasts to skillet; spoon sauce over chicken. Simmer, uncovered, for 5 minutes. Season to taste with vegetable salt. Sprinkle with parsley and serve immediately.

SERVINGS: 4. CALORIES PER SERVING: 185

SEAFOOD DIVAN

2 packages (10 ounces each) frozen broccoli
7 ounces freshly cooked crabmeat
6 ounces freshly cooked, cleaned shrimp
1 3/4 cups skim milk
1 tablespoon arrowroot
1/4 teaspoon vegetable salt
1 teaspoon butter buds
2 ounces feta cheese, shredded
Paprika to taste

Steam broccoli and arrange in a baking dish. Spoon seafood over broccoli and set aside.

Preheat oven to 400 degrees.

Combine 1/2 cup of the milk, the arrowroot, and vegetable salt in a bowl; mix well. Combine this mixture with remaining 1 1/4 cups milk and the butter buds. Cook, stirring, till thick and bubbly, then remove from heat. Add shredded feta cheese and stir to melt. Pour over seafood, covering completely. Sprinkle with paprika. Bake till hot, 20 to 25 minutes.

SERVINGS: 4. CALORIES PER SERVING: 215

Note: One 7 1/2 ounce can salt-free waterpack tuna, drained, can be substituted for the crabmeat; for the shrimp, substitute 6 ounces cooked turkey breast, cut in bite-size pieces.

In her behavior modification classes, Kircher distinguishes between satisfaction and gratification, stressing that *internal* rewards resulting from active behavior are preferrable to immediate and temporary *external* rewards such as eating. She teaches guests to reward positive behavior with simple pleasures such as enjoying nature or friendship. Other classes instruct guests on good food combinations—legumes with grains (Susie's Rice Dish features this combination), nuts, or seeds and vegetables with starches or proteins. Other recipes feature tofu, which is high in protein and combines well with fruits and vegetables.

SUSIE'S RICE DISH

3 1/2 cups water
1 cup brown rice
1/4 cup wild rice (optional)
1 medium-size onion, chopped
4 carrots, sliced
1/2 cup raisins
1/4 cup sunflower seeds (optional)
3/4 cup raw or roasted peanuts

Place brown rice and wild rice in water in a saucepan and let soak for 1 hour.

Bring rice and water to a boil, add onion and carrots, and continue to boil, covered, for 10 to 15 minutes. Remove from heat and add remaining ingredients. If necessary, add some more water. Let stand for 10 minutes and serve as a main dish with a green salad or as a side dish.

SERVINGS: 4. CALORIES PER SERVING: 78

SANS SOUCI TOFU DISH

1 medium-size onion, sliced
2 tablespoons diced celery
1 cup sliced fresh mushrooms
1/2 cup vegetable broth
1 large square tofu, crumbled
1/2 green bell pepper, seeded and grated
1 teaspoon chopped fresh dill
3 medium-size fresh, ripe tomatoes, peeled, seeded, and
    chopped
1 medium-size onion, minced
1/4 cup pimientoes
2 tablespoons sunflower seeds
Garnish: Chopped fresh parsley

Simmer onion, celery, and mushrooms in vegetable broth in
saucepan for 5 minutes. Stir in crumbled tofu and green
pepper, then sprinkle with dill.

To make sauce combine tomatoes, onion, pimientoes,
and sunflower seeds in a second saucepan. Heat, but do not
boil.

To serve, turn tofu mixture into 3 individual serving
dishes, top with tomato sauce, and sprinkle with parsley.

SERVINGS: 3. CALORIES PER SERVING: 85
Note: This goes well with a green salad and steamed
squash or broccoli.

BOB'S TOFU DESSERT WITH FRUIT SAUCE

1 cup plain low-fat yogurt
10 fresh or frozen strawberries
1 tablespoon honey
2 tablespoons frozen unsweetened apple juice concentrate,
    thawed

1/4 cup water
1/2 teaspoon vanilla extract
1/2 square tofu

Blend yogurt, strawberries, and honey in blender till smooth. Set aside.

Combine apple juice concentrate, water, and vanilla in a shallow dish. Cut tofu in 2 × 2 × 1-inch pieces and soak in vanilla-water mixture for a few minutes. Remove tofu to 2 individual serving dishes. Top with fruit sauce and serve.

SERVINGS: 2. CALORIES PER SERVING: 65

Kircher oversees guests' activities with discipline and love guests are likely to feel they are visiting a health-conscious friend in the country. Each guest exercises at his or her own pace. Kircher supervises, checking blood pressure and guarding against overexertion. Her European background is reflected in her charming hospitality and fitness know-how. And some of her recipes recall Old World kitchens—for example, her Musli (a Swiss dish), or Fraises aux Fraises.

MUSLI

2 cups plain low-fat yogurt
2 tablespoons rolled oats
2 tablespoons unprocessed bran
1 tablespoon flax seeds
2 tablespoons oat bran
1 tablespoon sunflower seeds
Low-calorie sweetener to taste
Fresh fruit of your choice, cut in cubes

Mix together all ingredients except fruit. Divide among 3 individual serving dishes and top with fruit.

SERVINGS: 3. CALORIES PER SERVING: 55

FRAISES AUX FRAISES

3 cups sliced fresh strawberries
1/2 cup orange juice
1 teaspoon rum extract
1 can (16 ounces) low-calorie unpeeled apricot halves,
    drained
1 tablespoon honey (optional)
Optional garnish: 1 kiwi, peeled and sliced

Combine strawberries, orange juice, and rum extract in
bowl. Cover and chill 1 hour.

Blend apricots in blender till smooth; you should have 1
cup apricot purée. Add honey and 1 cup of the strawberry
mixture; cover and blend till strawberries are just chopped.
Stir mixture into remaining strawberry mixture. Cover and
chill. Serve garnished with kiwi slices or as a sauce.

SERVINGS: 8. CALORIES PER SERVING: 66

Evenings at Sans Souci are festive. Guests relax together by
participating in songfests or talent contests; guest speakers
lecture on pertinent topics. The spa is near the charming old
town of Bellbrook, where guests can walk and enjoy the
ambiance of the early American era.

Typical of guests' reactions is this recent visitor's comment: "A glorious week . . . I am going home with less
weight and more knowledge . . . one of the most worthwhile
things I have done for myself in a long time!"

Rancho La Puerta

Founded in 1940 by the late Dr. Edmond Szekely, a European philosopher, and his wife, Deborah, Rancho La Puerta was planned as a no-frills health camp, an experiment in natural living.

Forty-five years and some 300,000 guests later, the ranch offers a low-key regimen of sport, exercise, and diet.

Confident of the value of an idea far ahead of its time, the Szekelys and their first guests lived in tents and lunched on goat cheese and raw grains. Kerosene lamps provided lighting, and hired hands cranked victrolas for exercise music. The fitness pioneers retired at dusk and rose at dawn, in harmony with nature's rhythms. They grew thinner and calmer as the peaceful days passed.

Today, the same spirit prevails at the ranch. Tents have been replaced by handsome villas, haciendas, and rancheras. Menus are more sophisticated, but still wholesome and natural. There are no telephones in the guests' rooms, no room service, no pressure, no pretensions. Morning and evening hikes into the Sierra Madres expose urban refugees to the magic of sunrise and sunset.

The ranch site in Tecate, Mexico, was chosen for its climate. The sun shines brightly an average of 341 days a year. Ocean breezes and an elevation of 2,000 feet keep the ranch cool in summer and free of smog all year round.

To take advantage of this healthful climate, two of the ten gyms at Rancho La Puerta are outside. The Ranch also has tennis and volleyball courts, a putting green, and a two-and-a-half-mile, twenty-station exercise course that winds through vineyards, gardens, and olive groves. Indoors, in addition to the gymnasiums, are saunas and whirlpools to soothe weary muscles. Massages and herbal wraps are also available. There are both indoor and outdoor pools.

Thirty optional exercise classes are scheduled each day. Some, like weight training, are for men only. The program is permissive—guests proceed at their pace. Beauty treatments are available—facials with Golden Door cosmetics, manicures, and pedicures. A wonderfully stocked library is open each evening. Guests can browse through classics or contemporary literature and listen to classical music. Other evening activities include lectures, classes, and movies.

Originally a vegetarian retreat, the spa now serves a modified vegetarian diet. Only organically grown fruits, vegetables, and grains are served, produced locally and picked at their prime whenever possible. Fish is served twice a week; and no preservatives, fats, or stimulants are used. Salads are popular fare at the Ranch, particularly make-your-own salad buffets or Mexican specialties like Spinach-Lettuce Salad Verde and Mexican Salad Cachanilla.

SPINACH-LETTUCE SALAD VERDE

1 small head romaine lettuce
1 bunch fresh spinach
8 cherry tomatoes, halved
8 small black olives

1 large onion, minced (marinated in 1/4 cup cider
    vinegar)
1/4 teaspoon Dijon mustard
1/8 teaspoon vegetable salt
1/8 teaspoon freshly ground black pepper
2 tablespoons basil vinegar
2 tablespoons olive oil

Trim, wash, and dry romaine and spinach. Combine with
tomatoes, olives, and onion.
    Combine remaining ingredients to make dressing. Pour
over salad. Toss well and serve at once.
    SERVINGS: 4. CALORIES PER SERVING: 17

MEXICAN SALAD CACHANILLA

1 head romaine lettuce
1/2 cup 1/4-inch-thick orange slices, peeled
1/2 cup 1/4-inch thick cucumber slices
1/2 cup 1/4-inch-thick jícama slices
1/4 cup chopped pecans
1/4 teaspoon Dijon mustard
2 tablespoons cider vinegar
1/4 teaspoon paprika
1 teaspoon honey
2 tablespoons olive oil

Trim, wash, and dry lettuce. Arrange in salad bowl. Add
orange, cucumber, jícama, and pecans. Mix remaining ingredients well and pour over the salad. Toss well and
serve.
    SERVINGS: 4. CALORIES PER SERVING: 120

Mexican food is served frequently, although many of the
dishes are very different from what Americans expect. Typi-

cal of the new Mexican Continental cuisine are Fish Rancho
La Puerta and Shrimp à la Muñoz.

FISH RANCHO LA PUERTA

8 fresh fish fillets
1/4 cup lemon juice
3 tablespoons vegetable salt
Freshly ground white pepper to taste
1 teaspoon corn oil margarine
1/2 clove garlic, finely chopped
2 teaspoons chopped shallot
1 medium-size leek (white part only), cut into
    julienne
16 carrot sticks, blanched
16 celery sticks, blanched
16 broccoli florets
1 cup dry white wine
2 1/2 cups plain low-fat yogurt
2 tablespoons Dijon mustard
Garnish: 1 teaspoon chopped fresh parsley

Briefly marinate fish in lemon juice, 2 tablespoons of the
vegetable salt, and pepper for 30 minutes.
    Preheat oven to 350 degrees.
    Melt margarine in a saucepan. Add garlic, shallot, and
leek; sauté 2 minutes. Add vegetable sticks and broccoli
florets. Stuff each fillet with vegetable mixture and roll up.
Place fish rolls in flameproof baking pan. Pour wine over.
Cover pan and bake 20 minutes. When done, remove fish
rolls and keep warm.
    On stovetop reduce cooking liquid to half. Add yogurt,
mustard, and remaining 1 tablespoon vegetable salt. Pour
sauce over fish rolls, sprinkle with parsley, and serve at
once.
    SERVINGS: 4. CALORIES PER SERVING: 184

SHRIMP À LA MUÑOZ

1/4 cup lemon juice
1 clove garlic, finely chopped
1 medium-size onion, sliced
3/4 cup sliced carrots
3/4 cup sliced celery
4 fresh parsley sprigs
2 bay leaves
1/8 teaspoon dried thyme
6 peppercorns
2 1/2 cups water
1/2 cup dry white wine
16 shrimp, shelled, deveined, and rinsed
1 1/2 cups plain low-fat yogurt
1 tablespoon Dijon mustard
1 teaspoon capers
3/4 teaspoon fresh tarragon or dried
2 tablespoons caviar

Marinate shrimp in lemon juice for 25 minutes.

Combine garlic, onion, carrots, celery, parsley, bay leaves, thyme, and peppercorns in a saucepan. Add water and wine and bring to a boil; simmer, uncovered, 15 minutes. Strain broth. Bring broth to boil again. Add shrimp and cook 5 minutes over medium heat. Remove from heat and cool shrimp in broth.

Make a sauce by combining yogurt, mustard, capers, tarragon, and parsley in a bowl. Drain shrimp and add to sauce, along with caviar. Mix well and serve at once.

SERVINGS: 4. CALORIES PER SERVING: 139

Because fresh seafood is plentiful in the area, Chef Carlos Muñoz Aguilar has created several fish and shrimp recipes. The traditional Veracruzano style of preparing seafood is an Aguilar specialty, as is Fish Soup Golfo.

FISH SOUP GOLFO

1 tablespoon olive oil
2 tablespoons chopped onion
1/4 clove garlic, finely chopped
2 tablespoons chopped green bell pepper
1/4 cup diced carrot
1/4 cup diced celery
1/4 cup diced potato
1/4 cup sliced fresh mushrooms
1/2 cup chopped tomato
3 cups Vegetable Broth (recipe follows)
1/8 teaspoon dried oregano
8 ounces fish fillet, cubed
2 tablespoons chopped fresh coriander (cilantro)
1 tablespoon Pernod liqueur

Heat oil in a saucepan. Add onion, garlic, green pepper, carrot, celery, potato, and mushrooms; sauté for 5 minutes. Add tomato, vegetable broth, and oregano; simmer, uncovered, 10 minutes. Add fish and coriander; simmer an additional 5 minutes. Serve soup in 4 individual soup bowls, with 1/2 teaspoon Pernod in each.

SERVINGS: 4. CALORIES PER SERVING: 111

VEGETABLE BROTH

2 cloves garlic, finely chopped
1 cup chopped onion
1 cup chopped celery
1 1/2 cups chopped carrots
1/2 cup chopped tomato
4 fresh parsley sprigs
2 bay leaves

1/4 teaspoon dried thyme
6 peppercorns
8 cups water

Combine ingredients in a saucepan. Bring to a boil. Reduce
heat and simmer, uncovered, 2 hours. Strain. Use for inclu-
sion in sauces and soups, or serve as a plain consommé.
MAKES ABOUT 4 CUPS. CALORIES PER CUP: 11

FISH FILLETS VERACRUZ STYLE

1 pound fish fillets
1 tablespoon plus 1/2 teaspoon vegetable salt
1/2 teaspoon lemon juice
1/2 teaspoon Worcestershire sauce
1/8 teaspoon freshly ground black pepper
1 tablespoon olive oil
1/2 cup sliced onion
1 clove garlic, finely chopped
1 green bell pepper, seeded and cut into
        julienne
4 cups peeled, seeded, and chopped tomatoes
1/2 cup tomato purée
1 teaspoon chopped fresh parsley
8 black olives, pitted and halved
1 tablespoon capers
1/4 teaspoon freshly ground black pepper

Place fish fillets in oven dish. Sprinkle with the 1 tablespoon
vegetable salt, lemon juice, Worcestershire sauce, and pepper. Set aside.
    Preheat oven to 350 degrees.
    Heat olive oil in a saucepan. Add onion, garlic, and green
pepper and sauté 3 minutes. Add tomatoes and tomato
purée; cook, uncovered, 5 minutes. Add parsley, olives, cap-

ers, the 1/4 teaspoon vegetable salt, and pepper; cook 1 minute more.

Pour sauce over fish. Cover dish with foil and bake 8 minutes. Serve immediately.

SERVINGS: 4. CALORIES PER SERVING: 253

SHRIMP VERACRUZ STYLE

Marinade:
1/4 cup lemon juice
1/8 teaspoon sea salt
1/4 teaspoon Worcestershire sauce
1/8 teaspoon freshly ground black pepper
1/2 teaspoon vegetable salt

Shrimp:
16 shrimp, shelled, deveined, and rinsed
2 tablespoons sesame-seed or safflower oil
1/2 teaspoon finely chopped garlic
1 cup chopped onion
1 cup chopped green bell pepper
1/2 cup tomato purée
3 cups peeled, seeded, and chopped tomatoes
1 teaspoon chopped fresh parsley
1/4 cup white wine
2 tablespoons chopped black olives
2 tablespoons capers

Pour marinade mixture over shrimp and let sit for 30 minutes.

Heat oil in a saucepan. Sauté shrimp 3 minutes. Add garlic, onion, and green pepper; sauté 2 minutes more. Add tomato purée, tomatoes, parsley, and wine; cook, uncovered,

for 10 minutes. Add olives and capers; cook an additional 2
minutes. Serve at once.

SERVINGS: 4. CALORIES PER SERVING: 187

Other ethnic delights are Tortilla Soup—invented by thrifty
Mexican cooks to use up leftover tortillas—and Stuffed
Chayote, and fruit concoctions like Pico de Gallo and Kiwi
Kuchumaa.

TORTILLA SOUP

3 ounces day-old corn tortilla, cut into strips
2 tablespoons safflower oil
1/2 clove garlic, finely chopped
1/2 cup chopped onion
2 cups seeded and chopped tomatoes
2 cups tomato purée
1 tablespoon chopped fresh mint leaves
4 cups Vegetable Broth (page 216)
1 cup cubed Monterey Jack cheese
2 tablespoons imitation bacon bits

Crisp tortilla pieces in oven, then sauté lightly in 1 tablespoon hot oil. Remove from skillet with slotted spoon and set
aside.

Heat remaining 1 tablespoon oil in skillet. Sauté garlic
and onion for 3 minutes. Add tomatoes, tomato purée, mint,
and vegetable broth. Cook, uncovered, over medium heat
for 15 minutes. Divide tortilla pieces, cheese, and bacon bits
equally among 4 or 8 soup dishes. Pour soup over and serve
at once.

SERVINGS: 4 TO 8. CALORIES PER SERVING: 132 TO 264

STUFFED CHAYOTE SQUASH

2 chayote squash, halved, peeled, seeded, and scooped out
    to accommodate stuffing
1 tablespoon safflower oil
1/4 clove garlic, finely chopped
2 tablespoons chopped onion
2 tablespoons chopped zucchini
2 tablespoons chopped pimiento
2 tablespoons chopped celery
1/4 cup Bechamel Sauce (recipe follows)
1 egg yolk
2 tablespoons grated Swiss cheese
1 1/2 teaspoons freshly grated Parmesan cheese

Cook scooped-out chayote in just enough water to cover for
10 minutes. Set aside.
    Heat oil in a saucepan. Sauté vegetables for 4 minutes.
Set aside. Preheat oven to 375 degrees.
    Combine thoroughly bechamel sauce, egg yolk, and
cheeses. Pour over sautéed vegetables; mix well. Stuff
chayote with mixture. Place in baking dish and bake for 10
minutes. Serve immediately, with rice.
    SERVINGS: 4. CALORIES PER SERVING: 98

BECHAMEL SAUCE

4 teaspoons arrowroot
1/4 cup cold water
1 cup low-fat milk
1/8 teaspoon freshly ground white pepper
1/8 teaspoon freshly grated nutmeg
1/4 teaspoon sea salt

Dissolve arrowroot in cold water. In saucepan combine remaining ingredients. Bring to a boil, then stir in arrowroot. Simmer mixture for 5 minutes.

MAKES 1 CUP. CALORIES PER CUP: 147

EGGPLANT PARMIGIANA

1 eggplant, cut into 1/2-inch-thick slices
1 teaspoon vegetable salt
4 egg whites, beaten
2 tablespoons olive oil
1 clove garlic, finely chopped
1/2 cup chopped onion
2 cups seeded and chopped tomatoes
1/4 cup tomato purée
1 bay leaf
1/4 teaspoon dried oregano
1 teaspoon chopped fresh parsley
1/4 teaspoon freshly ground black pepper
1 cup grated mozzarella cheese
2 tablespoons freshly grated Parmesan cheese

Sprinkle each eggplant slice with vegetable salt, then dip each into egg whites. Heat oil in a skillet and gently sauté each eggplant slice, one by one. Set aside. Add garlic and onion and sauté 3 minutes. Add tomato purée, bay leaf, oregano, parsley, and pepper. Simmer, uncovered, 10 minutes.

Preheat oven to 450 degrees.

Arrange eggplant slices in baking dish. Cover with sauce, first removing bay leaf. Sprinkle cheese over, then bake 10 minutes. Serve at once.

SERVINGS: 4. CALORIES PER SERVING: 223

PICO DE GALLO

1/2 cup cubed jícama
1/4 cup fresh squeezed orange juice (very sweet and
    full-flavored; see note below)
1/2 cup cubed fresh pineapple
1/2 cup cubed fresh papaya or melon
1 orange (very sweet and full-flavored; see note below),
    sliced
Chili powder to taste

On a platter, arrange jícama cubes, then pour over orange
juice. Place toothpicks in the cubes. Add the remaining fruit
cubes and the orange slices, placing toothpicks in some but
not all. (This will slow you down a bit while eating.) Sprinkle
with chili powder.

    SERVINGS: 4. CALORIES PER SERVING: 60
    Note: Mexican pineapples and papayas are different from
the Hawaiian variety, but any kind will work in Pico de Gallo
(which means "the rooster's beak") as long as you have the
proper orange and orange juice. In the words of a pico de
gallo aficionado, it must be the kind of orange that seems so
noncitric it almost "jumps right up at you and sweets you to
death." Do not add any sugar or gooey dressings, just chili
powder. Even if you believe you aren't going to like it, try
a light sprinkle. You may get addicted.

KIWI KUCHUMAA

1 cup plain low-fat yogurt
2 tablespoons honey
2 tablespoons orange juice
1 teaspoon vanilla extract
8 kiwi, peeled and sliced
Garnish: Fresh mint leaves

Combine thoroughly yogurt, honey, orange juice, and vanilla in a bowl. Add kiwi, toss to coat, and refrigerate 2 hours.

Serve in frosted sherbet glasses and decorate with mint leaves.

SERVINGS: 4. CALORIES PER SERVING: 100

PEAR WITH BLUEBERRIES

2 ripe pears, cored and halved
1 cup dry white wine
1/2 teaspoon vanilla extract
Pinch ground cloves
Pinch ground cinnamon
1/4 cup honey
1 cup fresh blueberries
2 tablespoons Grand Marnier liqueur

Combine pears, wine, vanilla, and spices in a saucepan; simmer, covered, for 8 minutes. Drain pears, reserving liquid, and arrange each half in an individual serving dish.

In another pan, heat honey. Add liquid in which pears cooked. Add blueberries; cook 3 minutes. Remove from heat, add Grand Marnier, and flame. Pour over pears, dividing equally, and serve immediately.

SERVINGS: 4. CALORIES PER SERVING: 145

VERSATILE MELON DESSERT

1 cup plain low-fat yogurt
2 tablespoons honey
2 tablespoons orange juice
1 teaspoon vanilla extract
8 ounces melon, peeled and sliced
Garnish: Fresh mint leaves

Combine thoroughly yogurt, honey, orange juice, and vanilla in a bowl. Add melon and toss to coat. Refrigerate 2 hours. Serve in frosted sherbet glasses and decorate with mint leaves.

SERVINGS: 4. CALORIES PER SERVING: 59

The excellent meals, the fitness programs, and the beautiful environment—all these are reasons why guests like Dr. Jonas Salk, Erma Bombeck, and William F. Buckley return to this resort. Some guests (Kim Novak, for instance) alternate between the Ranch and The Golden Door, Deborah Szekely's other, more expensive health resort, modeled after Rancho La Puerta.

The ranch facilities cover 125 acres; to maintain the high quality of its service a staff of 125 attends to the needs of a maximum of 125 guests—held to this number since 1960. The Ranch's aim is not to enlarge the facilities to accommodate more guests but to continually upgrade the diet and fitness programs in keeping with its motto—*Siempre Mejor,* always better!

Lake Austin Resort

W arm winds, wildflowers, water sports . . . in Texas? Lake Austin Resort, nestled in the famed Texas hill country next to the Colorado River, may be the best-kept secret of the South. Twenty miles from Austin, the center of the New Southwest's high-tech boom, the Resort is known for its unique blend of informality and sophistication. It offers peaceful seclusion and easy accessibility, combining a comprehensive approach to health, fitness, and relaxation with moderate prices and a beautiful natural setting.

Formerly a fishing village, and once a nudist colony, Lake Austin Resort provides guests the opportunity to tailor a fitness program to their own specific needs, with assistance from a staff of professional health educators, exercise physiologists and specialists, a nutritionist, and a registered nurse. More than twenty exercise classes are offered each day, from gentle stretching to vigorous workouts, from water aerobics to weight training to supervised early-morning walks through the hill country. All classes are optional; guests may participate in as many as they wish.

Facilities include glass-walled gyms overlooking Lake Austin, indoor and outdoor pools and Jacuzzi, a parcourse, hiking and jogging trails, a supervised weight room, paddle boats, and the lake itself. Guests have free use of the facilities, as well as constant opportunities for quiet contemplation in a serene outdoor environment.

Evening programs include special guest speakers on a variety of topics, new and classic movies, crafts, cooking and art classes, and the opportunity to socialize with new friends. Soothing massages, European facials, hair and nail care are available from a complete selection of grooming and beauty services, including an up-to-date boutique.

"Renewal" is the key word at Lake Austin Resort, which changed management in 1983. According to Cecilia Contini (formerly director of Rancho La Puerta): "Lake Austin is dedicated to providing a full-service fitness program at moderate prices. We offer an environment in which guests can lose their cares and find new energy and vitality." Tennis courts, an outdoor exercise pavilion, and an admissions building renovated to look like a turn-of-the-century Texas ranch house are in the works: "We want to tie the ambiance of this area to what we do here. By combining legendary Texas warmth and hospitality with the state's equally legendary 'can-do' attitude, we provide a really optimal environment for personal revitalization."

The Resort's dietary motto is "low-calorie cuisine for high-energy living." Toward this end, recipes low in sodium, fat, and sugar make up the 900- to 1,200-calorie regimen offered at Lake Austin. About a quarter of these calories are consumed at breakfast, where guests can choose fruits or juices; a small scoop of scrambled eggs; a tortilla, toast, or muffin; and/or a serving of the Lake Austin Resort Energy-to-Burn Breakfast.

APPLE-BRAN MUFFINS

2 cups unprocessed bran
1 cup rolled oats
1/4 cup whole-wheat flour

2 teaspoons ground cinnamon
1/4 cup sunflower seeds
2 eggs
1 cup buttermilk
1/4 cup molasses
2 large apples, cored, peeled, and cut in small chunks

Preheat oven to 400 degrees.
    Combine bran, oats, flour, and cinnamon in bowl; mix well. Combine in blender sunflower seeds, eggs, buttermilk, molasses, and apples; blend well. Pour blended ingredients into dry ingredients and mix just till dry ingredients are moistened. Spoon into 12-cup muffin tin and bake for 25 minutes.
    MAKES 12 MUFFINS. CALORIES PER MUFFIN: 60

LAKE AUSTIN RESORT ENERGY-TO-BURN BREAKFAST

2 cups quick-cooking oats
1/4 cup soy flour
3 cups raw wheat germ
1 cup unprocessed bran
1/4 cup vegetable oil
1/4 cup brown sugar, firmly packed
1 cup shelled sunflower seeds
1 cup raisins

Preheat oven to 325 degrees.
    Combine all ingredients except for sunflower seeds and raisins in bowl. Place in ungreased shallow baking dish and bake for 30 minutes, stirring once after 15 minutes. Remove from oven; stir in sunflower seeds and raisins. Cool and store in a covered container in the refrigerator for up to 1 week.
    MAKES 11 CUPS. CALORIES PER 1/4-CUP SERVING: 125

Male guests get their extra calories with a supplementary protein serving at lunch and an additional complex carbohydrate at dinner. Nondieters can request extra food. Meals are served in the lake-view dining room; the menu offers a wide variety of wholesome and delicious selections, like Artichoke-Mushroom Quiche, Fish and Asparagus Roll-ups, and Shrimp Stir-Fry, all suitable for dinner or lunch.

ARTICHOKE-MUSHROOM QUICHE

1 can (14 ounces) artichoke hearts
8 ounces fresh mushrooms, sliced
2 cups shredded Monterey Jack cheese
3 whole eggs plus 1 egg white
1 cup skim milk
1/8 teaspoon freshly ground black pepper
1/4 teaspoon dried basil
Paprika to taste

Preheat oven to 350 degrees.
   Drain artichokes, chop, and squeeze till barely moist. Place artichokes in quiche dish that has been lightly oiled with margarine.
   Sauté mushrooms in a dry pan and place on top of artichokes in quiche dish. Sprinkle with cheese.
   Beat eggs and egg white together; add milk, pepper, and basil. Pour mixture over cheese, then sprinkle with paprika. Bake for 40 minutes.
   Serve immediately.
   SERVINGS: 8. CALORIES PER SERVING: 160

VEGETABLE SOUP

2 celery stalks, trimmed and chopped
1 onion, minced
1 carrot, peeled and chopped
4 fresh, ripe tomatoes, quartered
1 head cabbage
2 bay leaves
2 tablespoons garlic powder
8 cups water
2 cups tomato purée

Combine all ingredients in stockpot. Bring slowly to a boil.
Simmer, covered, about 2 hours. Adjust seasonings as necces
sary.
SERVINGS: 8. CALORIES PER SERVING: 40

FISH AND ASPARAGUS ROLL-UPS

1 cup water
2 carrots, peeled and cut into 12 strips
15 ounces canned asparagus spears
6 flounder fillets (4 ounces each)
2 tablespoons margarine
1/2 teaspoon dried dillweed
1/4 teaspoon grated lemon zest

Preheat oven to 350 degrees.
Bring water to a boil in large saucepan. Add carrots.
Cover and simmer over medium heat about 10 minutes, or
till tender. Drain. Place carrot strips and asparagus spears
crosswise on top of fish fillets, dividing evenly among fillets.
Roll up and place seam sides down in baking pan.
In small bowl, combine margarine, dillweed, and lemon

zest. Brush mixture over fillets. Cover and bake for 20 to 25 minutes, or till fish flakes easily with a fork.

SERVINGS: 6. CALORIES PER SERVING: 70

SHRIMP STIR-FRY

1 tablespoon peanut oil
1/4 cup each diced green and red bell pepper
12 ounces shrimp, shelled, deveined, and rinsed
1/4 cup dry vermouth
1/2 cup fresh snow peas
1/2 cup julienne-cut carrots (matchstick pieces), steamed
   until tender-crisp
1 clove garlic, minced
1/2 cup sliced scallions

Heat oil in wok, over medium heat. Add peppers and stir-fry till tender, about 2 minutes. Add shrimp and stir constantly for about 2 minutes. Add vermouth and continue to stir-fry for another 2 minutes. Add snow peas, carrots, garlic, and scallions and cook till heated through. Serve immediately.

SERVINGS: 2. CALORIES PER SERVING: 275
Note: May be served over rice.

CORNISH GAME HEN À LA ORANGE

1 medium-size onion, sliced
2 Rock Cornish game hens, halved
1/2 teaspoon paprika
1/2 cup frozen orange juice concentrate, thawed
2 tablespoons chopped fresh parsley
1/2 teaspoon ground ginger
1/3 cup water

Preheat oven to 300 degrees.

Arrange onion slices over hens in a baking pan. Sprinkle with paprika. Combine remaining ingredients and pour over chicken and onions. Cover and bake for 1 hour.

SERVINGS: 4. CALORIES PER SERVING: 200

CHICKEN TERIYAKI

6 whole chicken breasts, skinned
3 cups dry white wine
3 cups Worcestershire sauce
1/4 cup ground ginger
1/4 cup garlic powder
3 shallots
1/4 cup frozen orange juice concentrate, thawed
2 tablespoons lemon juice
1 cup water
1 tablespoon freshly grated nutmeg

Preheat oven to 300 degrees.

Marinate skinned chicken breasts for 2 to 4 hours in the remaining ingredients, combined in a shallow glass dish.

Arrange chicken in 2 shallow pans; pour marinade over, dividing evenly. Cover and bake for 1 1/2 hours.

SERVINGS: 6. CALORIES PER SERVING: 190

CHICKEN IN WHITE WINE

1 tablespoon vegetable oil
1 whole chicken breast, skinned, boned, and halved
1 cup plus 2 teaspoons dry white wine
8 ounces fresh mushrooms, sliced
2 tablespoons minced onion
1 teaspoon dried tarragon
1 teaspoon arrowroot

Heat vegetable oil in a heavy skillet over medium heat till hot. Add chicken and brown on both sides. Add the 1 cup wine, mushrooms, and onion. Simmer, covered, for 15 minutes.

Remove chicken from skillet and keep warm. Add tarragon, arrowroot, and the 2 teaspoons wine to mushroom mixture in skillet. Cook, stirring constantly, till thick.

Pour sauce over chicken and serve immediately.

SERVINGS: 2. CALORIES PER SERVING: 220

ENCHILADA CASSEROLE

1 onion, chopped
1 clove garlic, minced
10 fresh mushrooms, sliced
2 green bell peppers, seeded and chopped
2 cups cooked kidney beans
1 1/2 cups seeded and diced tomatoes
1 tablespoon chili powder
1 teaspoon ground cumin
1 teaspoon ground red (cayenne) pepper
1/2 cup ricotta cheese
1/4 cup plain low-fat yogurt
6 corn tortillas
1/4 cup shredded Monterey Jack cheese

Preheat oven to 350 degrees.

Heat in a saucepan and sauté onion, garlic, mushrooms, and green peppers till tender. Add beans, tomatoes, and spices. Simmer, covered, over low heat for about 30 minutes.

Combine ricotta and yogurt. In a casserole dish sprayed with low-calorie vegetable coating, lay out tortillas and add sauce, 1 1/2 tablespoons of grated cheese, and 2 tablespoons of the cheese-yogurt mixture to each tortilla. Any extra sauce can be poured over the enchiladas. Bake for 15 minutes.

Serve immediately.

SERVINGS: 6. CALORIES PER SERVING: 180

PASTA PRIMAVERA

2 green bell peppers
2 red bell peppers
1 cup cauliflower florets
2 cups broccoli florets
2 medium-size zucchini
1 1/2 cups snow peas
1/4 cup olive oil
1 pound fresh mushrooms, sliced
1 tablespoon dried basil
1 pound pasta, cooked
2 tablespoons freshly grated Parmesan cheese

Blanch the green and red peppers briefly in boiling water. Drain, then peel, seed, and dice. Steam cauliflower, broccoli, and zucchini for 5 minutes; add the snow peas for the last minute.

Heat oil in a large skillet. Add mushrooms, peppers, and steamed vegetables and stir-fry for approximately 30 seconds. Add basil.

Toss vegetables with the cooked pasta. Divide among 4 serving plates; sprinkle each serving with 1 1/2 teaspoons Parmesan cheese. Serve immediately.

SERVINGS: 4. CALORIES PER SERVING: 250

YOGURT AMBROSIA

1/2 cup ricotta cheese
1/2 cup plain low-fat yogurt
20 seedless grapes
1 apple, cored
1 orange, peeled
1 ripe banana, peeled
1/2 honeydew melon, peeled and seeded
1/4 cantaloupe, peeled and seeded

Combine ricotta and yogurt. Dice fruits and place in a large bowl. Add ricotta-yogurt mixture and combine thoroughly. Chill.

SERVINGS: 8. CALORIES PER SERVING: 50

The atmosphere at Lake Austin Resort is informal; guests are served and supervised by a staff of up to fifty, but can set their own pace. The resort is open year round and can accommodate up to eighty persons. Special weeks for couples or management seminars can be scheduled.

SPA ADDRESSES

Bonaventure Resort Hotel and Spa
250 Racquet Club Road
Fort Lauderdale, Florida   33326
(305) 389-3300

Canyon Ranch
8600 East Rockliff Road
Tuscon Arizona   85715
(800) 742-9000

Four Seasons Hotel
1 Logan Square
Philadelphia, Pennsylvania   19103
(215) 564-4633

The Golden Door
P. O. Box 1567
Escondido, California   92025
(714) 744-5777

The Greenhouse
P. O. Box 1144
Arlington, Texas   76010
(817) 640–4000

The Heartland
180 North Michigan Avenue
Suite 1820
Chicago, Illinois   60601
(312) 236–2050

The International Health
and Beauty Spa at Gurney's Inn
Montauk, New York   11954
(516) 668–2345

La Costa Hotel and Resort
Rancho La Costa
Costa del Mar Road
Carlsbad, California   92008
(800) 854–6564

Lake Austin Resort
1705 Quinlan Road
Austin, Texas   78732
(512) 266–2444

National Institute of Fitness
Prospector Square
Box 1698
Park City, Utah   84060
(801) 628–3317

The Oaks
122 East Ojai Avenue
Ojai, California   93023
(805) 646–5573

The Palms
572 North Indian Avenue
Palm Springs, California   92262
(619) 325–1111

Pritikin Longetivity Center
1910 Ocean Front Walk
Santa Monica, California   90405
(213) 450–5433

Rancho La Puerta
Rancho La Puerta, Inc.
Tecate, California   92080
(619) 478–5341

Sans Souci
3745 West Franklin Road
Bellbrook, Ohio   45305
(513) 848–4851

The Spa at Palm-Aire
2501 Palm-Aire Drive North
Pompano Beach, Florida   33060
(800) 327–4960

The Wooden Door
P. O. Box 830
Barrington, Illinois   60010
(312) 382–2888

For further information on health spas,
you can write Health Travel International at
222 Wisconsin Avenue, Suite 6,
Lake Forest, Illinois 60045, or call
(312) 234–5652.

INDEX